PRACTICE LIKE THIS!

35 EFFECTIVE WAYS TO GET BETTER FASTER

JONATHAN HARNUM, PhD

Practice Like This! 35 Effective Ways to Get Better Faster
by Jonathan Harnum, PhD

Published by *Sol Ut Press*
Copyright ©2015 by Sol Ut Press and Jonathan Harnum. All rights reserved. No part of this book may be copied or reproduced by any means whatsoever without prior written permission of the publisher. Sol Ut and the Sol Ut logo are trademarks of *Sol Ut Press*.

Sol Ut Press is committed to education. **We have given away well over 1.5 million eBooks to students all over the world.** Get your own free digital copies of books on how to read music, jazz theory, and playing trumpet at www.sol-ut.com.

DISCOUNTS ON SOL UT BOOKS ARE AVAILABLE FOR PREMIUMS, SALES PROMOTIONS, AS WELL AS FOR FUND-RAISING, EDUCATIONAL, OR TEAM-BUILDING USE. SPECIAL EDITIONS OR BOOK EXCERPTS CAN BE CREATED TO YOUR SPECIFICATION.

FOR DETAILS, SEND INQUIRIES TO INFO@SOL-UT.COM.

GET FREE SUPPORTING MATERIAL FOR THIS BOOK
WWW.PRACTICELIKETHIS.COM

ISBN 10: 1-517676908
ISBN 13: 978-15176769-0-2
LCCN: 2015916409

PUBLISHER'S CATALOGING-IN-PUBLICATION

Harnum, Jonathan.
  Practice Like This! 35 Effective Ways to Get Better Faster / Jonathan Harnum, PhD.
  pages cm
  ISBN **0-970751225**

1. Self-actualization (Psychology). 2. Motivation. 3. Change (Psychology). 4. Life skills. 5. Time management. 6. Success. I. Title.

BF637.S4 H37 2015
158.1 --dc23   2015916409

FOR GARZA,
WHO WAS ASKING FOR IT.

CONTENTS

ABOUT THE BOOK 2

1: TALENT IS PRACTICE IN DISGUISE

THE THREE TYPES OF PRACTICE. 5
RIDE IT LIKE YOU STOLE IT 11
FAIL BETTER 13
STRATEGY VS. TECHNIQUE. 17
STYLIN' WITH MYELIN 19

2: MOTIVATION IS LIKE BREATHING (IT'S REQUIRED)

HUMILIATION POWER. 27
STEP INTO THE FOREVER BOX 29
10 MOTIVATION HACKS. 31
LOWER YOUR SIGHTS 35
GOALS & PRACTICE 36
ZIP YOUR LIPS. 41

3: YOU ARE UNIQUE (AND SO IS EVERYBODY ELSE)

YOUR SECRET BELIEFS 45
THE BLAME GAME 61
LEARNING Á LA MODE. 69
HEY! TEACHER! 73
MONKEY SEE, MONKEY DO 75

4: Time is The Most Valuable Thing You Spend

Speed Is Relative 79
The 10,000-hour Red Herring 81
Adopt Guerrilla Tactics 83
Good Morning, Sunshine 85
Stages of Mastery 87

5: Where You At?

Compass Over Maps 93
Mise en Place 95
Under the Influence 97
Group Practice 100
Find the Fast Lane 101

6: Do It To It

Tackling the Monster 107
The Practice Cycle 108
The Structure of a Great Practice Session 110
Check Yourself (Before you Wreck Yourself) 111
Creative Practice 115
All About the Benjamin 119
Going Mental 121
Chaining 123
Back-Chaining 126
Playing With Time 128
Let's Get Physical 131
Field of Dreams 133
At the Buzzer 138

We learn by practice. Whether it means to learn to dance by practicing dancing or to learn to live by practicing living, the principles are the same. One becomes in some area an athlete of God.

—Martha Graham

> We're all gonna die trying to get it right, so aim high, and aim true.
>
> —Vance Joy

ABOUT THE BOOK

Don't Tell Me What to Do!

This book is designed to be read however you like. Cruise straight through it or skip to a topic whenever your interest or need arises. You'll find lots of cross-references pointing to related information to help with cherry-picking, if you want to jump around.

The Six Sections of the Book

SECTION ONE: What it means to get better, and how it works in the brain.

SECTION TWO: Getting and staying motivated to improve.

SECTION THREE: Covers way your unspoken theories about talent shape your practice, and also how others can help you get better faster.

SECTION FOUR: Tackles time and practice, including how much, what time of day, and how your practice needs change over time.

SECTION FIVE: Where you practice and who you practice with will both increase how quickly you improve.

SECTION SIX: Contains specific strategies, techniques and information to help you squeeze the most juice out of your practice time.

Get Better Faster isn't meant to be comprehensive; these are just the best tips, tricks, mindsets and strategies I haven't seen covered together elsewhere. In many cases, in order to keep things short and sweet, you'll get just a taste, and it'll be up to you to dig deeper. Cool?

Plan to Scan: One Way to Dig Deeper

With a smart phone or tablet and a QR reader, you can see, hear, and read more on a particular topic. *Scan* is a great QR reader. You can download the app for free to any phone or device at https://scan.me/download.

If you're reading this on a Web-connected device, click on the HTML address to go to the extra information. You can always enter the Web address into a browser. I've shortened them to make this easier.

Get the Full Color PDF

Get your free copy of the hyperlinked, full-color PDF by scanning this QR code, or point your favorite Web browser to http://www.PracticeLikeThis.com/FreePDF

ONE

Talent Prac

> ## In This Section
> ---
> The 3 types of practice, the benefits of thievery, failing with purpose, and your brain on practice.

IS TICE IN DISGUISE

The Three Types of Practice

Accidental Practice

Play as Practice

Intentional Practice

The 3 Types of Practice

Talent is practice in disguise, and practice is more than you think. There are three kinds of practice. One you're probably familiar with, but the other two aren't usually considered practice. They are, I assure you.

"Natural ability" is a convincing illusion. When we see Danny Way jump the Great Wall of China on a skateboard with a broken ankle, it's easy to assume "natural talent" plays a part in his awesome ability because we can't see the thousands of hours of practice (and injuries!) that Danny Way put in to earn such incredible skills.

With very few exceptions (like height in basketball players), a great deal of research has shown that natural ability is mostly an illusion. At the very least, practice plays more of a role than genetics. Two kinds of practice contribute to the illusion of natural talent. I call them "accidental practice" and "play as practice." Talent is practice in disguise.

There are other illusions surrounding practice. One is that practice is boring and tedious. It can be, of course, but I've spoken with dozens of world-class professionals, and *every one of them* says they *enjoy* practice. It's fun! That's not to say practice isn't challenging and difficult, of course. It's all in how you approach practice, and how you define it, too. Speaking of which, let's take a look at the three types of practice.

> *There are three kinds of people: Those who make it happen, those who watch it happen, and those who wonder what happened.*

ACCIDENTAL PRACTICE

In 1920, developmental biologist Zing Yang Kuo rubbed warm Vaseline over fertilized chicken eggs. Kuo suspected that a chick's ability to peck wasn't genetic, but was a *learned* ability, a radical idea at the time. The Vaseline made the eggshell translucent so Kuo could peep in on the chicks' development. What he found was astonishing.

When the chick's heart began to beat, the tiny bird was packed so tightly inside the shell that it's little beak rested directly above its heart. Kuo saw that the thumping heartbeat moved the chick's beak in the "exact same motion" the chick would use for pecking. The chick was *practicing* the motion before it even hatched. This is accidental practice: unconscious practice that takes place because of your surroundings.

In India it's known as *samskar*, or unconscious influence on ability. It's about the only time the word "gift" makes sense when you're talking about skill. Accidental practice is what you absorb unconsciously from your environment, often—but not always—as a child. Extreme skiing legend Shane McConkey started skiing at 23 months. At three years old, he rode in a front-facing pack while his mom skied. His view unobstructed, Little Shane would exhort her to do jumps. That's *samskar*. McConkey was one of the greatest athletes to have walked (and flown) the earth. Check out his epic skills in the excellent documentary of his life at http://www.mcconkeymovie.com.

The good news is that *samskar* isn't absolutely necessary if you want to become great at something. Talent is simply practice in disguise. The secret to getting ahead is getting started, the sooner the better.

START NOW.
IN JUST 2 DAYS,
TOMORROW WILL BE
YESTERDAY.

Play is often talked about as if it were a relief from serious learning. But...play IS serious learning.

— Mister Rogers

PLAY AS PRACTICE

There is a deep connection between play and learning. The Latin word *ludus* means "school," but it also means "play." The connection isn't coincidental. Play is often the best way to learn, especially at first.

Babies and animals use play to learn, but you can harness it, too. For some musicians, especially pop, punk, and folk musicians, this is the only kind of practice they use to get better. I've spoken with internationally touring musicians who have told me, "I never practice." It's not true, though. Their practice is *play*: learning songs, writing songs, playing with friends, performing, messing around, etc. She didn't say it to me, but Sonic Youth bass player Kim Gordon said it best: "There's a real art to not learning how to play an instrument and being able to still play it."

Practice-as-play is how many sports legends have built up tons of practice as kids. You can get very, very good using this method, with the added bonus that it's fun. Without a bunch of time spent just messing around, Tiger Woods would never be able to do this: http://is.gd/elexix.

The fastest way to get better is up next.

Intentional practice (also known as deliberate practice) is the Big Daddy of getting better, and the focus of this book. When you practice—or play—with focused intent on improving, your progress is *much* more rapid. Check out this helpful video explaining this kind of practice at http://is.gd/sidezo.

We're going to dig deeply into all three of these kinds of practice for the rest of the book, but we'll give extra attention to intentional practice, because it's the best way to improve quickly. With these techniques, you'll continue to improve at what you love for the rest of your life.

You ready?

> A CAREER IS BORN IN PUBLIC—
> TALENT, IN PRIVACY.
>
> — MARILYN MONROE

Ride It Like You Stole It

Steal any idea you can wrap your larcenous mind around if it's going to help you get better. When you steal ideas, you have to ride them hard if you want to tweak them into a shape that fits your particular needs.

Try everything you come across in this book (and anywhere else), but interrogate these ideas. Make them give up their secrets. Discover both how they *will* work for you, and how they *won't*. Here are some questions to ask about any improvement strategy:

1 - Does this sound like it'll work for me? How exactly? If it won't work, why not?
2 - Do I need help understanding or implementing this? Who can I ask? What does Google have to say about it?
3 - How can I tweak this approach to work for me?
4 - What's the opposite of this idea?
5 - Can I combine this with something else?
6 - If I took this approach to an extreme, what would it look like?
7 - What's the absolute bare minimum I could get away with, using this approach?
8 - Is this an idea and a way of thinking, or is it something I would actually *do*? Does that change how I use it?
9 - How can I apply this to what I'm working on and my level of skill?
10 - Can I safely ignore this information? Why?
11 - Am I thinking too hard about all this instead of just jumping in and getting on with it?

> *Good artists copy; great artists steal.*
> — Steve Jobs

THE OBSTACLE IS THE PATH (handwritten)

FAIL BETTER

Become familiar with failure. If you're like most people, this will be one of the more difficult challenges you face on your path to awesome. Nobody likes to fail. Nobody. But what separates the masters from the mediocre is their attitude toward failure.

Without a keen awareness of your failures—however big or small they might be—you won't know what needs work. Punk rock legend Mike Watt said it like this: "You need bad things to make good things. It's like with farming—if you want to grow a good crop, you need a lot of manure." For a healthy dose of inspiration, check out some of the world's greatest "failures" at http://is.gd/ceyapi.

When we care deeply about doing something well, failure can be a blow, but with the right attitude, it's a blow that will propel you forward, not crush you. We'll get to why that is and how you can adopt the right attitude later in the book.

Masters in every field treat mistakes as useful feedback. Jazz trumpet legend Dizzy Gillespie's horn was bent upwards accidentally, but Dizzy *liked* it that way. It's an iconic image along with his giant puffed cheeks. Dizzy quipped, "I decided I liked the horn bent because I can hear a note the minute I hit it. This way I can hear my mistakes faster."

If failure ever makes you want to quit, think of it like "dying" in a super fun video game: sure, it's annoying, frustrating, and sometimes even embarrassing or infuriating, but are you going to let that stop you from finishing the level, defeating the boss? Of course not. You reboot and rally. You find a way.

An important fact that's easy to forget is that if it were easy, it would be boring. The obstacle *is* the path. Make that your mantra.

SUCCESS
FAILURE

Success is moving from one failure to another with no loss of enthusiasm.

—Winston Churchill

So Now What Do You Do?

1 - **Look for failure!** Seriously. You have to actively seek out your weaknesses, your failures, so you can correct them. Nobody's perfect, so you *do* have these flaws, even if you're not trying to find them. Find them! Get help from someone better than you who can perceive errors you can't see.
2 - **Don't beat yourself up,** and don't take the failure (or yourself) too seriously. Failure is a learning opportunity. If you have a hard time with this one, learn why starting on page 45.
3 - **How do you feel, and why?** It's normal to feel embarrassed, angry, hurt, and a whole range of other not-so-pleasant emotions when you fail. Don't shrink back from those emotions, they're a sign you care. Explore them. Those powerful feelings help you identify what needs work. What doesn't kill you makes you stronger.
4 - **What happened?** Take a good, long, unflinching look at what happened. Who or what was the reason for the failure? For help, see *The Blame Game* on page 61.
5 - **What are you going to do about it?** A failure is great, because it gives you a concrete goal to work on. Draw up a battle plan to attack the reasons behind the failure, and don't be shy about getting help in any way possible: YouTube, Google, or best of all, someone with more experience than you who is a good teacher or coach. Learn more about the right kind of teacher for you on page 73.
6 - **Remind yourself that the obstacle is the path.** Obstacles are what you see when you take your eyes off the goal. Michael Jordan said, "I've missed more than 9,000 shots in my career. I've lost almost 300 games. Twenty-six times I've been trusted to take the game winning shot and missed. I've failed over and over and over again in my life. And *that* is why I succeed."

Strategy vs. Technique

A strategy is an approach anybody can use. A technique is the skill necessary to get the most juice out of a strategy. Let's use the example of failing better in your practice to explain the difference between a strategy and a technique.

Failing better means correcting errors the moment you notice them during practice. That's the strategy: correcting the error as soon as you notice it. Anybody can do it. The *technique*—the skill the strategy requires—is being able to *spot* the error. If you can't see the error, or hear it or smell it or taste it or whatever, you can't fix it.

This concept is illustrated in the highly unscientific "clam graph" to the right. Why clams? In some circles, a clam is slang for a mistake. These clams, however, do *not* taste good, even when deep-fried.

The greater your ability and awareness become, the finer your error-detection skills will be, and the more clams you'll catch.

Superb athletes, musicians, writers, and others, no matter how advanced their skills, are always on the lookout for errors. Nobody's perfect. Perceiving error is a skill. A glitch Derek Jeter might see in his swing is probably a detail that almost nobody else would catch. Get it?

No matter what skill level you're at, from beginner to expert, strive to detect more and more subtle errors in what you're doing. Then find the right strategy and get rid of those clams. Permanently.

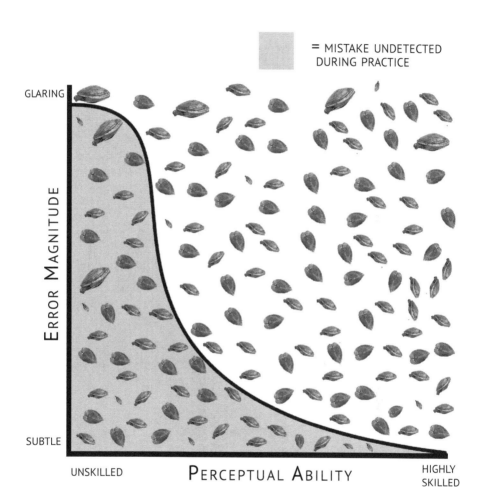

Stylin' with Myelin

To change your body, you must first change your mind.

Your Plastic Brain

Your brain is plastic in the good sense of the word, meaning it changes based on its surroundings. Myelin is one thing that changes in the brain when you learn a new skill. Whether you're swinging a club, throwing a ball, fingering a fiddle, crafting a succulent bouillabaisse, sculpting clay, or doing *any* physical activity, you need myelin to perform that task well.

Myelin—first described by Rudolph Vicrow in 1854—is a fatty insulator that coats the axons connecting the millions of neurons used to perform any action. Myelin allows neurons to fire with greater precision, speed, and efficiency. Special cells—Schwann cells—deposit myelin on axons that receive regular use. Accomplished violin players have more myelin surrounding the neurons that control their left hand, making that part of their brains significantly bigger than non-violin players.

There are two important things to know if you want to harness the power of myelin to get better faster. The first is that Schwann cells deposit myelin *very* slowly, like growth rings in a tree. It's gonna take time. Channel the tortoise. The second thing to know is that myelin is a mindless process. Those little Schwann cells will deposit myelin on a neuron *even if what you're doing is wrong*! That's the crucial detail.

When you're learning a new skill, you *have* to go slowly enough to perform the skill well, because you have to build the connections that reinforce accuracy. Careful practice makes perfect. You *must* stay alert for errors and fix them immediately so you don't encode bad habits. Schwann cells that deposit myelin inside your brain are mindless and mechanical, so you have to be smart. This is the essential difference between the brain (the mechanical jelly in your head) and the mind (your consciousness).

Check out this colored image of a myelinated nerve taken by Steve Gschmeissner with a scanning electron microscope. On the Web at http://is.gd/imowep.

The diagram on the next page will help you understand myelin better.

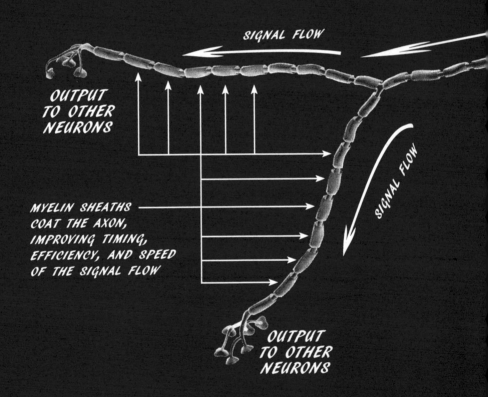

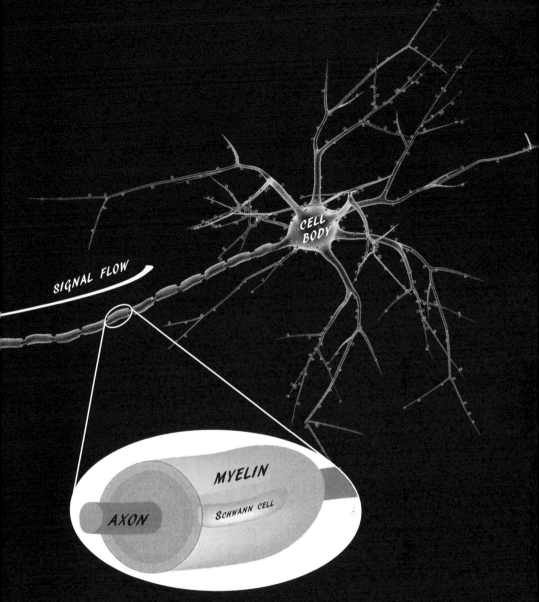

So Now What Do You Do?

1 - **Can you go slowly**, even with a skill you do well? It might be harder than you think. How slowly are you able to perform the skill accurately? You'll probably find that going *that* slowly is a challenge at first. Do it. You'll get better.
2 - **Are you performing all the actions** necessary to make what you're doing correct? This can cover a *lot* of details. Musicians and actors must consider tone quality, emotion, and tempo, to name a few specifics. Are you nailing *all* the details necessary for accuracy and artistry? If not, go slower until you can.
3 - **Simplify.** Perhaps you're trying to do too much at once (as in #2). Can you isolate one single aspect of the skill, maybe a particular motion (or emotion). Practice *only* that at a very slow speed until you can execute that one thing without error. Gradually add complexity.
4 - **Watch a master perform** the same skill very slowly. Live is best, but slowing down video will work, too. Study it.
5 - **Stare with all your senses** to avoid errors. This relates to #2 above. When you're practicing slowly like this, especially if it's a complex task, it will help to record yourself now and then. When an error crops up, attack it immediately and persistently until it's gone. If the error happens again, you're probably going too fast. Slow down more.
6 - **Get some help** from a teacher, coach, or some other highly qualified person who knows what they're doing and will give you useful feedback. Even a knowledgeable friend can give you useful feedback.

> You'll never make a mistake
> if you never make a mistake.
>
> — Julius Baker

TWO

MOTIVA

IS

> **IN THIS SECTION**
>
> MOTIVATION HACKS: TIPS, TRICKS, AND MINDSETS TO KEEP YOUR HEAD IN THE GAME & GROWING SKILLS.

TION

LIKE

BREATHING

(IT'S REQUIRED)

Humiliation Power

There is power in humiliation, and you can see evidence of it all over the place: Michael Jordan not making the cut for his varsity basketball team; Steve Jobs and NeXT computers (or LISA); Charlie Parker laughed off the bandstand for losing his place in the music at a jam session; the list is endless.

Humiliation is an awful emotion to feel, an experience I only wish on my worst enemies, and jerks in general. It's not fun at all, and therein lies humiliation's power.

When you fail publicly, the humiliation that comes from such a failure can be a *huge* motivator to get better. The catch is that you have to have the right attitude.

If you're pushing your own boundaries, and if you care what others think of you, you're bound to experience humiliation at some point in your life. The good thing is that humiliation itself won't kill you. If you're an extreme athlete, however, the humiliation won't kill you, but the mistake might, so take this advice with a grain of salt if your ambition is to jump off cliffs or out of airplanes.

Humiliation is relative: some feel it more than others. Whether it's at the local open mic or at a Superbowl halftime show, the feeling is real. If you feel humiliated for a failure, *use* that powerful emotion as motivation to work extra hard so it never happens again.

Take comfort from the fact that you're not alone. Justin Timberlake quotes both Steve Jobs and Teddy Roosevelt to reinforce the power of humiliation and the strength to deal with its challenges. Timberlake's talk is at http://is.gd/rabatu.

The problem is not the problem. The problem is your attitude about the problem.

Do you understand?

Captain Jack Sparrow

Step Into the Forever Box

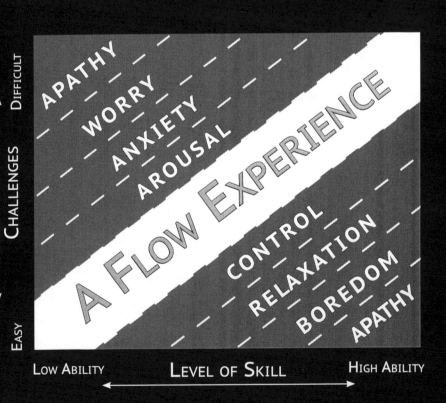

Stand-up comics call it the forever box, but this state of being many names—the deep now, the groove, the zone—and it's the most powerful motivator you can experience. Researchers call "Flow," a term coined and extensively researched by psychologist Mihály Csíkszentmihályi (MEE-hy Cheek-sent-MEE-hy).

Csíkszentmihályi interviewed world-class experts, but he also talked to Navajo sheep-farmers, teenage Japanese motorcycle gang members, and many others. He found Flow is a powerful source of happiness, and Flow improves performance and productivity. A Flow state is a *powerful* motivator for continued improvement. Why is the Flow state so powerful?

The chemicals released by the brain in a Flow state include some of the most powerful psychoactive "reward chemicals" naturally produced by the brain: norepinephrine (speed), dopamine (cocaine), anandamide (THC), endorphins (opiates), and serotonin (MDMA).

The Flow state is its own reward. Because Flow feels better than just about anything, Flow provides *serious* motivation to get more of it. The difference between illicit drugs and Flow-state chemicals is that in Flow, the chemicals are naturally produced by the brain, with the added bonus that you won't be thrown in jail for experiencing the high. Once you sample it, you'll want more of it. I know *I* do.

This is a deep topic that deserves more space than we've got here. Check out Steven Kotler's *The Rise of Superman,* and his six videos at http://is.gd/yasana. They're captivating and worth watching. Kotler has identified 17 triggers that will help you get into a Flow state. He divides the triggers into 4 categories:

1 - **INTERNAL TRIGGERS (3):** States of mind that keep you focused on the present moment. One of these is the ability-to-difficulty ratio, illustrated in the diagram to the left. Flow happens when your abilities perfectly match your challenge.
2 - **EXTERNAL TRIGGERS (3):** Surroundings that force you into a Flow state.
3 - **SOCIAL TRIGGERS (10):** Being with others can trigger group Flow in team-related activities.
4 - **CREATIVE TRIGGER (1):** A creative approach triggers Flow, and Flow increases creativity in a feedback loop.

10 Motivation Hacks

1 - **Start now.** Don't wait for the perfect tool, the perfect mood, the perfect instrument, the perfect business plan, the perfect coach, the perfect whatever. The sooner you start—even if it's a tiny start—the better.

2 - **Just show up.** Writers and artists know this one. You have to be in the chair, or in the studio, or in the office in order to get work done, even if (especially if!) you don't feel like doing it. Showing up is more than half the battle. Michael Jackson's producer Quincy Jones called it Ass Power: the ability to keep your butt in the chair and get work done. Jones said Ass Power was the ability that separated MJ from equally talented musicians Jones produced.

3 - **Get happy.** Happy people procrastinate less. To get happier, try gratitude, giving back, savoring, encouraging your optimism, and celebrating progress (see #4 below).

4 - **Set small goals.** Small, easily achieved goals make progress easier and more visible. Harvard psychologist Teresa Amabile's research found that when you're aware of progress, you're significantly more motivated. New York Times bestselling author Brent Weeks starts his novels with the tiny goal of writing only 250 words per day (there are 381 words on this page). More on goals is up next.

5 - **Leave it out.** Whatever tool it is you use to get better (a ball, a glove, a club, a knife, an instrument, etc.), leave it out and readily available. Those quick bursts of practice add up, and there is solid evidence that time-staggered practice is better than one long practice session.

6 - **Kill your boredom!** If you find yourself becoming bored, *do* something about it. Get creative, shake things up, take off your shoes and socks, or something equally simple or silly that shocks you out of your routine. Clark Terry inspired me to turn my trumpet upside down and practice scales by pushing the valves up with the backs of my knuckles. Much less boring.

7 - **Go Live.** Go see live people, doing what you love, in the flesh, and get as close as you can to them without being a weirdo or a creep about it. If you're unsure whether you *are* being a weirdo or a creep in these situations, you probably are. Err on the side of caution.

There are only two days in the year on which nothing can be done. The first is called yesterday and the other is called tomorrow; so today is the right day to love, believe, do, and mostly, live.

— Dalai Lama

Don't quit. Suffer now and live the rest of your life as a champion.

Muhammad Ali

8 - **Co-mingle.** Join a group of like-minded folks who talk and exchange ideas about your chosen skill. This is particularly good advice for people like writers or solo musicians who spend a lot of time alone (believe me, I know about this one!). Get-togethers can be online of course, but live is better. With cookies, if possible.

9 - **Avoid a rewards mentality.** There is clear research evidence from educational psychologist Edward Deci and many others that for most tasks, rewards actually make you perform *worse*! Focus on mastery of the task, not some external reward like a gold star, a trophy, adulation, or cash. Learn more about this important topic from one of many delightful RSA animations—this one done from a talk by Daniel Pink—at http://is.gd/nitixu.

10 - **Never give up.** Tenacity is your most valuable asset. Researchers like Angela Duckworth and have found that "grit" was more important than talent in achieving success. Check out her talk about grit at http://is.gd/lajawu. Long-time Chicago Symphony bass-trombonist Ed Kleinhammer said, "World-class trombone players do not just happen. Their talents are forged in the dual furnaces of determination and diligence."

As an example of epic tenacity, I present "Daily" Dale Webster. In 1975 he decided to surf every day for a full lunar cycle. Over 28 ½ years later—10,407 days—through illness and storms, he succeeded. Doesn't get much grittier than that. Check out Daily Dale's story at http://is.gd/rulodu.

Lower Your Sights

Goals act as a compass and a guide, but it can be hard to know exactly what you need to practice to achieve your goals, especially your long-term goals.

Research shows us that actually *achieving* a goal helps motivation, and since it's the shorter goals that add up to the long-term goals, those are the ones to focus on. Goals are like the Sierpinsky fractal to the right. They resemble and relate to each other at every scale.

You probably know about ultimate- and long-term goals, and it's a good idea to write out these biggies once or twice a year.

We know about short-term goals, too, but these aren't small enough, either. A short-term goal might be a week or a month away.

The smaller the goal, the more powerful it is because of its motivational power when you successfully complete it. For a real sense of progress, focus on even smaller goals: immediate, micro-, and nano-goals. These are the goals of a single practice session.

Check out the diagram to the right, with a brief explanation of each kind of goal on the following page.

Sierpinsky Fractal

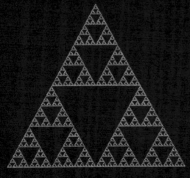

A fractal is a shape that repeats itself at every scale. That's why it makes such a good analogy for goals, which are also self-referential at different scales.

The fractal pattern was first described by Polish mathematician Wacław Sierpiński in 1915, but the design appeared in art much earlier.

GOALS & PRACTICE

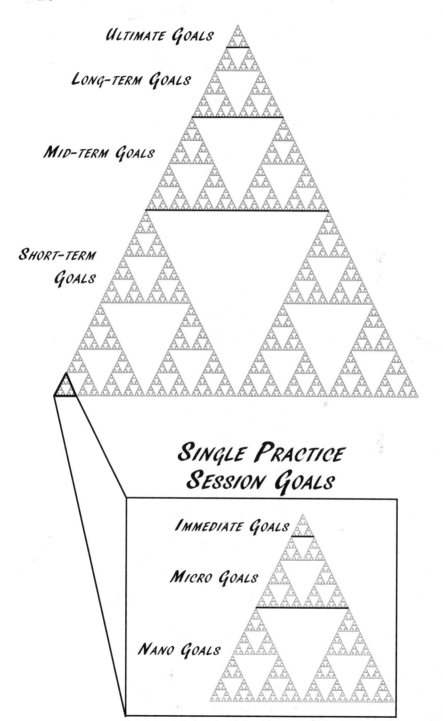

ULTIMATE GOALS: Your life's work. These will take years to accomplish, probably a decade or even more. Dream big. Write these goals down and revisit them once every year or three. Revise as needed.

LONG-TERM GOALS: These are still pretty long-term, maybe a five-year plan. Again, write them down and revisit them every six months or so.

MID-TERM GOALS: These goals are a year or six months out, and now we're getting into the realm of concrete things you want to learn: memorize the top 10 opening chess moves, learn all the diminished scales and how they're used, improve your putting game, investigate all marketing channels for your product, perform a full set of music, shave off time in your race of choice. Again, keep the goals in your mind, write them down, revisit and revise as necessary. Most importantly, use these goals to shape all smaller goals.

SHORT-TERM GOALS: Now you're getting to something you can actually *do* when you practice: fix that backswing, memorize the Ruy Lopez opening move in chess, learn the $A^\flat$ diminished scale. Again, make these goals relate to the longer-term goals. Make them measurable. Be specific.

IMMEDIATE GOALS: The goal of a single practice session. Keep it simple, short, and aligned with how much time you have to practice. Think small. Control your putting speed; learn why the 16th-century Ruy Lopez opening chess move is also called *The Spanish Torture*; memorize a pattern using the $A^\flat$ diminished scale.

MICRO GOALS: Think smaller. Break that immediate goal down into two or more parts that you can practice separately. Focus on the upper body and shoulders while putting; learn the Morphy defense to *The Spanish Torture*; drill the awkward fingering between 2 notes in the $A^\flat$ diminished scale. For two strategies to get even more oomph out of micro-goals, see chaining and back-chaining, starting on page 123.

NANO GOALS: One perfect repetition. That's your smallest goal. When you achieve it—and with attention you will—savor the accomplishment because that will fuel your motivation to continue.

> Vision without action is a dream. Action without vision is a nightmare.
>
> — Suman Sandillya

What you get by achieving your goals is not as important as what you become by achieving your goals.

Henry David Thoreau

So now what do you do?

1. **Keep it real, reachable, and measurable.** Howatt's research found that those who make their goals concrete and achievable are 50 percent more likely to be confident the goals will be attained, and 32 percent more likely to feel in control of their lives. Be as specific as you can: "Be awesome," is too vague and doesn't give you any kind of path to follow. "Learn the backstroke flip turn," is specific, short, measurable, and you'll know when you've achieved it.
2. **Keep track.** Write down your goals in a practice journal or your blog or somewhere. Start big and move toward the smaller goals, and as you do, connect them. What do your ultimate goals require from the shorter-term goals? The act of writing out your goals will help you think through exactly what you want and what you need to do. Post them in a prominent place to remind yourself.
3. **Talk through your goals** with a more experienced person, like a teacher, coach, mentor, or even a more experienced friend. They'll help you focus in on what you need, what you're missing, and what to do next.
4. **Be sensitive** about setting goals, especially the little ones. The motivational guru with the coolest name ever, Zig Zigler, said, "A goal properly set is halfway reached." Achieving goals feels good, and will motivate you to continue. For smaller goals, choose easy targets.
5. **Don't obsess** over the countless goals you can dream up. If you itemized every triangle in that Sierpinsky fractal you'd go bonkers because they never end. At some point—the sooner the better—just get to work.

Great acts are made up of small deeds.

Lao Tzu

Zip Your Lips

Our large, luscious brains are good at imagining realities that don't exist. Researchers like Peter Gollwitzer have found that when you receive praise for your goals, your brain makes you feel like you've already accomplished them. Because of this, your motivation to actually *do* what you said you were going to do dries up. Because your brain takes this praise as evidence of accomplishment, you go catch the latest Simpsons episode, or goof off some other way instead of practicing. Stupid brain.

By all means, *do* set goals. But if you *must* blather on about them, make those you tell hold you accountable in some way. Give them permission to remind, cajole, and—if necessary—harass you if you don't make progress. That might counter-act your big brain's tendency to take the praise you receive when you state your goals and make you feel you've accomplished them.

One way to keep your goals in plain view would be to sign up over at www.GiveIt100.com and post a 10-second video each day for 100 days to chart your progress toward your goals.

There isn't much I have to say that I wouldn't rather just shut up and do.

Ani DiFranco

THREE

You

> ### IN THIS SECTION
> YOUR UNSPOKEN BELIEFS, PERSONAL TRAITS, AND CAREFULLY CHOSEN OTHERS WILL INFLUENCE HOW FAST (AND IF!) YOU GET BETTER.

Are Unique

(and so is everybody else)

Your Secret Beliefs

Even if you've never thought about it before, you hold certain beliefs about the nature of talent and intelligence, and these beliefs fundamentally influence how you approach learning.

Here's how it works: Some people believe intelligence is fixed, or set: you have a certain amount of smarts (like an IQ score), and that's all you get; you're either smart or you're not. Others believe intelligence is more fluid, that you can get smarter, improving your IQ score through effort and learning. In a now-famous (and often repeated) experiment, Dr. Carol Dweck showed that even *one sentence* of praise on either your intelligence or your effort profoundly changes how you approach a task.

Those praised for their *smarts* tend to have a "fixed" mindset, which fosters ego-based motivation (the left side of the diagram on the facing page). With a fixed mindset, intelligence becomes a fundamental part of one's identity. Someone with a fixed mindset is *highly* likely to avoid challenges, because failure is evidence you aren't smart, you don't have what it takes. It's a blow to the ego. We all want to protect our ego.

Those praised for their *effort* tend to have a "growth" mindset, which fosters mastery-based motivation (the right side of the diagram). Those with a growth mindset believe intelligence changes, so it's not as tightly bound up into your sense of self. For folks with a growth mindset, failure doesn't mean you're fundamentally untalented or stupid, just that you need to learn more, try again and maybe try harder, or do something different. A growth mindset results in more robust learning and a higher level of motivation, especially for challenging tasks.

There is a wonderful summary of Dr. Dweck's work from coach and trainer Trevor Ragan at http://is.gd/ohokep.

Research from Bret Smith has shown that our ideas about talent work the same way. If you think talent is genetic, then you have a fixed mindset, which deeply affects how you approach getting better.

To the right are the basics, and on the following pages you'll see how each mindset impacts how you approach challenges, obstacles, effort, critique, the success of others, and your overall progress.

The Two Faces of Belief About Talent

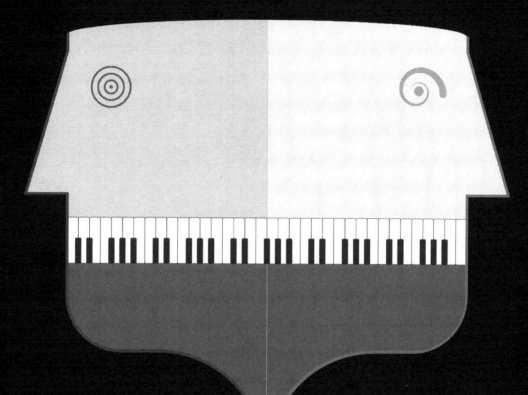

Fixed Mindset

You either have it or you don't. If you believe this, it fuels your desire to look like you "have it" and avoid any indication that you "don't have it."

Growth Mindset

Talent is grown over time through exposure and effort. If you believe this, it stokes your desire to learn. You persist, go deeper, and have more fun.

Each belief impacts your approach to learning, shown on the following pages.

WITH THIS MINDSET...

...YOU TEND TO SEEK AND EMBRACE CHALLENGES. YOU SAY, "I DON'T WANT TO FAIL, BUT WHEN I DO, I LEARN SOMETHING USEFUL. WHEN I TACKLE A BIG CHALLENGE, EVEN IF I FAIL, MY TALENT GROWS."

...YOU TEND TO AVOID CHALLENGES. YOU OFTEN TELL YOURSELF, "THAT'S TOO HARD." YOU FEEL THAT IF YOU FAIL, IT MEANS YOU DON'T HAVE TALENT, AND YOU DON'T WANT TO RISK ANYBODY SEEING THAT. YOU TEND TO STICK TO EASIER TASKS YOU CAN DO, PROVING YOU'RE TALENTED.

With this mindset...

...you tend to keep at it when the going gets tough. You often say, "I should look at this from another angle, try another approach, or see what others have done with a similar problem. I'll figure this out eventually."

...you don't really like obstacles, because if you're talented, there wouldn't be obstacles. If you get stuck on something, you tend to think it's evidence you don't have talent. You tend to give up easily, or seek tasks with few or no obstacles.

With this mindset...

...you tend to believe that effort means progress. You probably believe that the harder you work, the better you get.

...you tend to believe that if you have to put forth a lot of effort (or any effort), it's a sign you don't have talent. You prefer to take on tasks you know will be easy, so it looks like you have talent.

WITH THIS MINDSET...

...YOU TEND TO SEEK OUT INFORMED CRITIQUE, AND TELL YOURSELF, "WHAT CAN I LEARN FROM THIS PERSON'S OPINION?"

...YOU TEND TO AVOID ANY KIND OF CRITICISM, ESPECIALLY FROM AN EXPERT. YOU TEND TO BELIEVE THAT IF THERE'S SOMETHING WRONG WITH WHAT YOU'RE DOING, IT'S EVIDENCE THAT YOU DON'T HAVE TALENT.

WITH THIS MINDSET...

...YOU ENJOY AND FOLLOW THE SUCCESS OF OTHERS. YOU MIGHT SAY, "THAT'S AWESOME, I WANT TO DO **THAT!**"

...THE SUCCESS OF OTHERS MAKES YOU FEEL UNCOMFORTABLE, BECAUSE IT'S A SIGN THAT THEY HAVE MORE TALENT THAN YOU. YOU MIGHT FIND YOURSELF SAYING, "THEY'RE SO TALENTED! I COULD NEVER DO **THAT.**"

WITH THIS MINDSET...

...you'll continue to improve your whole life. At age 90, the world-famous cellist Pablo Casals was asked why he still practiced. He replied, "Because I think I'm making progress."

...you'll tend to plateau early, or quit. Those who do continue to get better often don't enjoy the process, and may be riddled with anxiety, guilt, and resentment.

Changing Your Mind

If you're like me, you don't have either a fixed or a growth mindset, but some messy combination of the two. There are things you can do to move toward having a more growth-oriented mindset. There's no special trick, but it will take awareness and some effort. It's like Bob Marley said: "None but ourself can free our mind." Here are some suggestions:

1 - **Imagine a scenario in the past** when you were either judged harshly or roundly praised for your ability. Whether painful or pleasant, feel it fully, using a fixed mindset. Now adopt a growth mindset and look at that scenario again. Did it change? What can you learn from that experience? Move forward.
2 - **Be hyper-aware of praise or criticism for talent,** especially from your inner critic. Change that talent-based praise into effort-based praise, even if it's only in your mind. Encourage your teachers and coaches to do the same.
3 - **Be aware of how you feel** when you encounter an obstacle or a big challenge. Do you want to give up? Run away? Ask yourself what you're really trying to avoid. Imagine three ways to tackle the challenge. Do them.
4 - **When—not if—you make a mistake,** how do you feel about it? Like a talentless hack? A loser? Does the mistake make you feel you don't have talent? Does it make you feel like you need to try harder or learn more? Put that mistake at the top of your list for focus in the next practice session.
5 - **Adopt the mindset of the eager novice**, no matter how good you might already be. Try to learn something every time you practice. Zen master D. T. Suzuki said it best: "In the beginner's mind there are many possibilities; in the expert's mind there are few." As you gain more and more skill, try to maintain the mind of a fascinated beginner.

> Progress is impossible without change, and those who cannot change their minds cannot change anything.
>
> —George Bernard Shaw

The Blame Game

The Usefulness of Blame

Blame is important, but not because you need a scapegoat so you don't feel guilty for your mistakes. *Anything* but that! Placing blame is helpful because it'll give you clues on where to focus your energy during practice. If you know where the fault lies, you can get busy tackling the problem.

There are only 3 questions you need to ask to get to the root of the cause and get to work fixing it. Each of the following will be explained on the next few pages.

1 - **Is the cause internal or external?** Basically, is it your fault, or the fault of something or someone else?
2 - **Is the cause constant or does it change?** A constant cause of error (like physics) can't be changed, but a variable cause of error (like lack of effort), *can* be changed.
3 - **Can the cause be controlled?** What can you *do* about the source of the error? Something like luck can't be controlled, but the difficulty of the task and level of effort can be controlled.

Placing blame so you can fix a problem can be a challenge. Reality is tricky and never as simple as we wish, which means that for any failure, the *exact* cause can be hard to see. Another challenge is accepting blame for failures that occur. But that's exactly what you need to do.

> *To play a wrong note is insignificant. To play without passion is inexcusable.*
>
> **Beethoven**

Locus: It's Not You, It's Me

Failure can be blamed on either an internal or an external cause, which is to say it's either your fault, or somebody or something else's fault. It shouldn't come as a surprise if the actual breakdown is a mix of both internal and external causes.

But here's the kicker: most people who become great at what they do tend to see the cause of a failure as internal; they tend to take responsibility for *any* error that occurs. Why?

If you perceive the cause of a failure as external, like bad weather, there may be little you can do to fix it. But if you perceive the cause for failure as internal, like not going out in bad weather, and therefore your own responsibility, you can do something about it.

Whether the cause is internal or external, whether you can do anything to fix the problem depends on how stable the cause of the failure is, covered on the next pages.

It's never the room's fault; it's never the equipment's fault; it's never the mouthpiece's fault; it's never anything but us.

— Wynton Marsalis

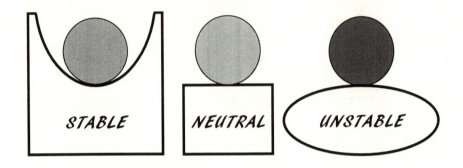

Stability

If the cause of a failure changes over time, it's an unstable, or variable cause; if the cause remains the same over time, it's a stable cause. Some causes are neutral, neither stable or unstable.

For example, if you think a lack of "natural" talent is a cause for your failures, you won't be motivated to change, because you believe talent to be a genetic source of ability, and you can't do anything about it short of science-fiction-style gene therapy.

However, if you see talent as it really is—changeable—you'll be more likely to persist at improving whatever talent you desire. You'll get better and better because you know effort grows talent.

A neutral cause is trickier. For example, you might be skeptical that talent is *only* practice in disguise: you believe there is such a thing as natural ability, but you also believe you can grow talent. That's neutral. The good news with neutral is that it still gives you some wiggle room to improve the outcome.

Whether a cause is constant, neutral, or variable, you still might not be able to change it. That's where control comes in.

Control

Control asks whether there is anything you can do about the situation. Some things—like luck or your current ability—are totally beyond your control: nothing you can do about it. What you *can* control is how much effort and thought you're putting into your task, as well as the difficulty of the tasks you choose. You either try harder, work smarter, or make the task easier. Here are a few suggestions for controlling a difficult task:

1 - **Slow down.**
2 - **Simplify.**
3 - **Take a smaller bite:** Maybe you're trying to do too much. Break down a complex task and work on a small chunk at a time. See page 123-129 for strategies.
4 - **Try a different approach.**
5 - **Get some help.** Why re-invent the wheel? Ask an expert.

And here's the crucial detail: successful people in all fields tend to see otherwise arbitrary causes of failure as controllable. This means successful people tend to believe the cause for the failure *can* be improved through effort, even if it seems impossible. Despite Yoda's famous advice, you *have* to try.

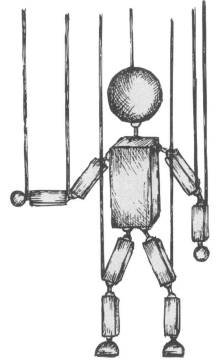

If you could kick the butt of the person who is the cause of all your problems, you wouldn't be able to sit down for a week.

So, what do you do?

1 - **Remember:** the goal is to get better, so leave your ego at the door. Accepting blame doesn't feel good, but taking ownership of an error means you can *do* something about it. Find out what, and do it.

2 - **Beware the seduction of placing blame elsewhere.** Escaping blame is a tendency that runs deep, so watch out! Assume you have some role in the failure. Find it. Fight it.

3 - **Internal or external?** When failure occurs (and it will occur, make no mistake), was the cause internal or external or both? Be specific and unflinching in your assessment.

4 - **Constant or changeable?** When failure occurs, is the cause constant or changeable? If it seems to be constant, find a chink in that armor. If it's changeable, how will you change it for the better? Do it.

5 - **Controllable or uncontrollable?** When failure occurs, can the cause be controlled? What can you do to keep it from happening again? Think big (think small, too). Act.

6 - **Get some feedback** from a coach, teacher, or other expert whose opinion you trust. No matter how good you are, there are always important details you're missing. Get help finding them.

7 - **Record it:** If you don't have access to a coach, make a recording: video, audio, whatever makes sense. Chefs will have a tough time with this one until someone invents a way to record smell and taste.

8 - **Seek more information** about the power of placing blame. What I've presented here are just surface details. Deepen your understanding at http://is.gd/otuhav.

9 - **Remember rule #6:** The story goes like this: a yoga teacher is working with a class when the door bursts open and a student rushes in, shouting, "I understand Rule #6!" and then rushes out. The teacher smiles, saying nothing. A student asks, "What is Rule #6?" The teacher answers, "Don't take yourself too seriously." The class ponders this in silence for a while. Then a bright student asks, "What are rules number one through five?" The teacher answers, "There are no other rules. Just that one."

Learning à la Mode

> The illiterate of the future will not be the person who cannot read. It will be the person who does not know how to learn.
>
> — Alvin Toffler

There isn't any scientific evidence that we each have a preferred learning style, but knowing about learning styles will help you pick up skills faster, better, and embed them more deeply. How? Use as many modes of learning as you can in your practice. Focus especially on the learning style that makes the most sense for the task at hand.

If you're learning how to kick a ball, hearing someone kick a ball (aural learning) won't help much, but *doing* it will (kinesthetic learning), and *watching* others kick the ball (visual learning) will help you learn how, too. You'll also want to use other styles, like reading about kicking the ball. Here are the basic learning styles most of us are familiar with:

KINESTHETIC: learning through gestures, body movement, object manipulation and positioning. Learning by doing.

VISUAL: learning through pictures, shapes, sculpture, or drawings. Learning by watching.

AURAL/ORAL: learning by sound, rhythm, tone, singing, and chanting. Learning by listening.

GUSTATORY: I made this one up, because chefs, sommeliers, and other food artists aren't quite covered with the three familiar styles above. This sense has to do with learning through taste, smell, and mouth feel.

MIX-AND-MATCH

A good example of how learning styles combine in real learning is how you learned to read and write. You used all the modes: visual (looking at letters), aural/oral (saying the letters and singing the alphabet song), and kinesthetic (writing out the letters). This is practice using different learning styles, all of which adds up to being able to read and write.

You may have to use *all* of these styles to learn most skills deeply, but you might find you have a preference for one learning style in particular, or one that makes more sense than the others for a certain task. During practice, see how many learning styles it makes sense to incorporate.

The model on the following pages—developed by David A. Kolb—highlights four general ways of experiencing the world, and those combine into individual learning modes. See if you recognize your preferred method in Kolb's learning modes on the next two pages. How might you tackle what you want to learn using other modes?

According to Kolb, the general preferences of learners tend to be:

1 - CONCRETE EXPERIENCE: DOING TASKS
2 - REFLECTIVE OBSERVATION: WATCHING AND THINKING
3 - ABSTRACT CONCEPTUALIZATION: THINKING
4 - ACTIVE EXPERIMENTATION: TRYING DIFFERENT APPROACHES

Taking these four basic types of learning styles, Kolb combines them to create a more nuanced picture of individual learning styles. Again, find the one that you most identify with, but use them all depending on what it is you're trying to learn.

Accomodaters

CONCRETE EXPERIENCER + ACTIVE EXPERIMENTER. YOU...
...PREFER HANDS-ON AND CONCRETE TASKS.
...WANT TO "DO."
...ENJOY DISCOVERY.
...ARE ABLE TO SET OBJECTIVES AND SCHEDULES.
...FEARLESSLY ASK QUESTIONS.
...ARE NOT AFRAID TO CHALLENGE THEORIES.
...ARE ADAPTABLE.
...LIKE TO RECEIVE INFORMATION FROM OTHERS.
...ARE APT TO GO WITH GUT FEELINGS RATHER THAN LOGIC.

Converger

ABSTRACT CONCEPTUALIZER + ACTIVE EXPERIMENTER. YOU...
...PREFER HANDS-ON AND THEORY.
...ENJOY ANALOGIES.
...PREFER SPECIFIC PROBLEMS.
...LIKE TO TESTS HYPOTHESES.
...STRIVE TO FIND THE BEST ANSWER.
...PREFER WORKING ALONE.
...ENJOY PROBLEM SOLVING.
...VALUE THE TECHNICAL OVER THE INTERPERSONAL.

Diverger
Concrete Experiencer + Reflective Observer. You...

- ...like real life experience and discussion.
- ...tend to be imaginative.
- ...know there is more than one possible solution.
- ...enjoy brainstorming and group work.
- ...would rather observe than do, at first.
- ...like having alternatives.
- ...like to have background information.

Assimilator
Abstract Conceptualizer + Reflective Observer. You...

- ...like theories and facts.
- ...enjoy theoretical models and graphs.
- ...like to talk about rationales rather than doing.
- ...believe lectures are a good way for you to learn.
- ...enjoy working with numbers.
- ...like to define problems.
- ...prefer logical formats.

You probably identify with one of these modes more than another, but if you're faced with a tough problem, look through this list of traits and find the ones that seem like they'd be useful for your particular task. Don't just stick with the methods that are most comfortable or most familiar. Choose the learning styles that push your awareness and ability to new levels.

> *One who would learn to fly some day must first learn to stand and walk and run and climb and dance; one cannot fly into flying.*
>
> — Friedrich Nietzsche

Hey! Teacher!
or
Put Me In, Coach!

Dr. Byrnes? I want to thank you for mentoring me.

In 1985 Dr. Benjamin Bloom and his team published several important studies on excellence. One researcher, Lauren Sosniak, found that world-class experts had three different kinds of teachers, each providing a style of teaching necessary for particular stages of development. If you're looking for a good teacher or coach, consider what Sosniak found.

Phase One Teachers & Coaches: Beginner

These teachers are usually close by, often in the neighborhood. More importantly, these teachers are playful and make lessons or practice fun. Any time the student shows aptitude, curiosity, or involvement, these teachers give lots of rewards and encouragement. Phase One teachers are less worried about correctness than they are about sustaining interest and enthusiasm; they emphasize playful involvement and exploration.

Phase Two Teachers & Coaches: Intermediate

Teachers in this stage are more formal, and teacher involvement often extends well beyond the lesson or practice time. These teachers convince students to take part in public demonstrations of their developing skill. They also arrange for students to spend time with like-minded people, and often help the student connect with professionals who are doing the same thing.

These teachers are more critical, rational, and systematic in their assessment of the student. Instead of praise and rewards, these teachers give the student tips, tricks, and pointers about how to get better. The relationship moves from fondness to one of respect and admiration.

Phase Three Teachers & Coaches: Advanced

In this phase, there is no longer such a close personal relationship (though there certainly can be). What matters most is the shared dedication to the field of study (music, sport, business, etc.). These mentors often have national or international reputations and are widely acclaimed for their excellence. They spend little or no time on basics, instead focusing on nuances, abstractions, expert-level critique, and stellar performance.

Something to Remember

A great teacher, coach, or mentor can *seriously* speed up your progress, but remember what Dr. Seuss said, "You can get help from teachers, but you're going to have to learn a lot by yourself, sitting alone in a room."

Mirror Neurons

The same neurons that fire in someone's brain when they do something will also fire in your own brain when you simply *watch* them do it! They're called mirror neurons, and like many important scientific discoveries, they were discovered by accident.

Monkeys in the lab of neurophysiologist Giacomo Rizzolatti were wired up so scientists could discover which parts of the brain were active when the monkey picked up a peanut. During a break, the monkey—still wired up—watched closely as a researcher picked up and ate one of the peanuts. Everyone was shocked when they saw the *same neurons* fire in the monkey's brain as she merely watched the researcher pick up the peanut. Learn more at http://is.gd/ikoyiz.

After lots of further research, scientists discovered that we humans have another mirror neuron system that encodes not only the task, but *how* the task is done. Watch and learn, indeed! More on using imitation in practice is on page 120.

Find a Top Model

Mirror neurons are one reason why it's absolutely *crucial* that you watch masters perform—in a live setting if possible—because even simply watching them is training your brain. The more familiar you are with a task, the more of your own neurons fire when you watch someone else do it.

When you watch, strive to take in everything you see, hear, smell, touch, and taste. Vary your focus as you watch: spend some time focused on big, overall picture, and then zoom in to scrutinize a fine detail. Do it live if you can. YouTube is great source, because you can slow things down by 50%, and use the infinite loop to watch over and over and over as you absorb those skills. Seeing is learning.

FOUR

TIME:

> **IN THIS SECTION**
> TIME AND PRACTICE: COVERS NOT ONLY HOW MUCH, TIME OF DAY, AND HOW LONG, BUT ALSO HOW GOOD PRACTICE CHANGES OVER TIME.

The Most Valuable Thing you spend

Speed Is Relative

Remember what Einstein taught us: speed and motion are relative.

Using the tips from this book, you're going to be like the turtle over there. Anybody who's fumbling along trying to figure things out on their own is like the snail. To them, your improvement will be blazing fast, nearly unbelievable!

To you, your progress might still seem slow. The deep kind of improvement you're after will take weeks, months, years, and maybe even decades. That's how it works, and you probably knew that, I just wanted to make sure.

Researchers like Angela Duckworth have found that "grit" is more important than any kind of "natural" ability. Tennis great Billie Jean King once said, "Champions keep playing until they get it right."

Remember that story about the tortoise and the hare? Slow and steady wins the race. The key is not giving up.

Einstein developed a theory about space, and it was about time, too.

The 10,000-hour Red Herring

by Donald Fraser: http://is.gd/dugoxi

You've all heard it by now: the 10,000 hour "rule," uncovered by Anders Ericsson and his colleagues in a 1993 study. Basically, they found that it takes around 10,000 hours of deliberate practice to reach expert-level performance, whether it's in sports, music, chess, comedy, x-ray diagnostics, or anything else. But the 10,000-hour rule is a red herring for lots of reasons. Here are a few:

1 - **Quality over quantity:** It's not the hours you practice, it's the practice in your hours. If you're practicing in the wrong way, or practicing the wrong things, it doesn't matter how many hours you put in. Quality of practice matters most. For an in-depth exploration of this liberating idea, check out Daniel Goleman's *Focus: The Hidden Driver of Excellence*, at http://is.gd/iwaxot.

2 - **World Class Performers:** This "rule" pertains to elite-level performers. You *do not* need 10,000 hours to be good (or even excellent), enjoy yourself, and entertain others. Josh Kaufman explores this in his book, *The First 20 Hours: How to Learn Anything Fast*, at http://is.gd/larumi.

3 - **Stay in the present moment:** Trying to wrap your mind around putting in 10,000 hours—which takes bout 10 years—is daunting. Forget about 10,000 hours and worry about the half-hour practice session you're going to do *today*. The future will take care of itself. Expert-level performers aren't trying to accumulate 10,000 hours, they're doing what they love to do, intensely focused on the task.

4 - **Context matters:** Time you spend with experts matters, too. Cultivate relationships with like-minded people to boost your ability more quickly. Does this sound familiar?

5 - **Beyond practice:** The 10,000 hour "rule" was coined by Ericsson to describe what he called *deliberate practice*. *All* experts do all sorts of other things that also contribute to their skills: performing, talking through things, messing around informally, reading, studying theory, watching others, watching YouTube videos, and many, many, many other activities. It all contributes. Greatness isn't about the hours, it's a lifestyle.

6 - **Don't practice practice, practice performance:** Legendary Chicago Symphony trumpeter Bud Herseth had some wise words of caution about practice. Herseth said, "You have to be careful about practice, or you start practicing practice. You need to practice performance." Even when you practice, whatever your practice is, imagine it's the performance. That way you'll be ready for the real thing when it's time.

Adopt Guerrilla Tactics

Guerrilla Practice

A regular fighter loses if she does not win; a guerrilla fighter wins if she does not lose. Adopt that attitude. Small strategic strikes are effective over time. Persist.

A guerrilla fighter is a member of a small independent group (that's you), fighting against a larger, regular force (that's every distraction that pulls you away from your dream). Guerrilla fighting is all about passion, David vs. Goliath odds, nimble movement, precise attacks, and limited resources, driving a DIY approach.

It's a mistake to think you have to set aside an hour or more of practice. That attitude causes a lot of busy people—which is all of us—to give up on practice altogether. You can do a lot in a 5-minute burst of practice. Even 2 minutes can be enough, as master teacher Hans Jensen demonstrated with one of his students who was learning a very difficult cello etude. She only had 2 minutes of time a day to spare (at first, they started at one minute, then doubled her practice time). It took her 6 weeks, but she mastered the piece.

Randomly distributed short bursts of practice might even be better than one long session. A Nobel prize-winning piece of research involving shocking sea snails found that brief experiences repeated at random intervals get more solidly packed into long-term memory than a regularly repeated experience. For more tips on harnessing the power of guerrilla practice, check out page 95.

Remember those tiny, micro- and nano-goals back on page 36? Pick one tiny thing: gripping a ball just so, a flick of the wrist, a rhythm, an elevator pitch to a potential angel investor: something small enough that you might get in several repetitions in a few minutes. When you have some down time, *do it!* It adds up.

Good Morning, Sunshine

You have limited brain power. As the day wears on, your ability to focus, to remember, and to learn weakens. That's why mornings or after a nap are the best times to practice.

The pros know this. In the study that spawned the 10,000 hour rule and the term *deliberate practice*, most of the elite performers studied did the bulk of their practice in the morning hours.

Now, if you need to practice your rifle marksmanship you can't really do that at 5 a.m., but there are some things you *can* do no matter what you're practicing. Here are a few:

1 - **TAKE TIME TO WAKE UP.** The first couple hours of the morning are usually the most productive, but not right away. For me, coffee is necessary. Give yourself an hour to wake up, then dive in. I've been experimenting with a pretty good 24-minute wake-up routine over at http://is.gd/yadeya. Tweak as necessary.
2 - **DECIDE WHAT MATTERS.** Once the day starts, we're bombarded by everybody else's needs. Take some morning time to decide from one to three things that are crucial for *you* to achieve today. Make a plan on how to achieve that and get to work.
3 - **ESTABLISH A ROUTINE.** Routines help prevent procrastination. So do places. USC psychologist Wendy Woods found that places trigger routines, often without the conscious mind getting involved. My own writing routine trigger is opening my office door (preferably with a cup of coffee in my hand) and firing up the computer.
4 - **CHOOSE WISELY.** If your chosen practice is something loud, like playing trumpet, you can still benefit from early practice, just choose some quieter aspect that can be worked on in the morning hours, like mental practice, which you'll learn about on page 121.

I firmly believe that every hour you practice before 10 a.m. is worth two hours later on.

Rex Martin

Stages of Mastery

These stages of a mastery are drawn from martial arts, but they can be applied to anything you're trying to improve. Each stage has particular needs to address and skills to acquire. Let's jump in.

Unconscious Incompetence

This is where most beginners start. You have no idea how bad you are, and like the saying goes, what you don't know can't hurt you. This is probably the most enjoyable phase because you're get to explore and play around and you don't take things too seriously.

The risk in this stage is that you might overestimate your skills because you can't perceive what you don't know. Remember the ability to perceive errors in the clam graph on page 18? It's like that. Here are other things to strive for as a beginner in this stage, whatever age you are:

1 - **Enjoy yourself and have fun.**
2 - **Explore what it means to be "good."** Closely watch masters in this field do their thing. How do you differ from them? What do they know that you don't know? What do they do that you don't?
3 - **Find some guidance**, preferably from phase one teachers—page 74—who work well for people in this stage.
4 - **To get out** of this stage, you've got to be more aware of the skills you should improve, and chip away at them. See #2 above for help.
5 - **Don't be so quick to get out** of this phase (or to push your kids out of it, parents). It's fun, and that enjoyment will go a *long* way towards enjoyment, satisfaction, and lifelong participation.

Conscious Incompetence

To paraphrase science fiction wizard Arthur C. Clarke, "Any sufficiently advanced ability is indistinguishable from magic." In this stage, you begin to realize what it takes to be really good. The Conscious Incompetence phase is the most unpleasant of the four, and alas, it's usually the longest. Realizing you have a lot to practice can be a blow to the ego, especially if you believe talent is something you either have or you don't. For a reminder about the power of a growth mindset, review page 45 to page 59. Here's what to focus on in this stage:

1 - **Keep up your motivation and attitude** by celebrating your progress. Set small, achievable goals so progress is easier to see.
2 - **Comparing yourself** to others is great. Beating yourself up because you're not Steve Jobs, Shania Twain, Michael Jordan, Serena

Williams, or any other star is not helpful. Keep your perspective.

3 - **IT'S EASY TO GET STUCK** in this stage, as many do. Moving out of it is as much a matter of gaining skill as it is a mental game.

4 - **WORK HARD. WORK SMART. BE PATIENT.** Eyes on the prize. Social psychiatrist Emily Balcetis found that those who focus intently on the finish line perceive the distance to it shorter than those who don't.

Conscious Competence

Now you're getting somewhere. It should be obvious that these phases don't follow in lock-step. You'll dip into and out of this phase early and often on your journey. Again, it's a matter of chipping away at your weaknesses so you achieve your reasonable goals. In this phase, you're aware of what it means to be competent, and you're aware of the kind of practice you need to do in order to reach that competence. In this phase, you're striving for:

1 - **GREATER MASTERY** of your chosen skill.

2 - **FREQUENT HIGH-LEVEL ASSESSMENT** from skilled people whose opinions you trust and respect. Like phase 3 teachers on page 74.

3 - **OPPORTUNITIES TO PERFORM** your skill, whatever that means: games, concerts, banquets, matches, etc. Anywhere and everywhere.

4 - **WAYS TO PUSH** your skills to the next level. It's easy to rest on your laurels. Strive to learn, grow, and be more effective.

Unconscious Competence

This phase is the realm of elite performance. We've all known this phase where language is concerned. Recall a long conversation with a great friend, when the words flow effortlessly. This is unconscious competence. The specifics of syntax, the tyranny of grammar—none of those details matter because we've absorbed them to the point that we can converse without conscious thought.

So much practice has been put in that thought is no longer necessary, and can actually get in the way of performing at peak levels. Here are some goals for those at this level:

1 - **STAYING IN "FLOW"** while performing. For a review, see page 29.

2 - **SKILL MAINTENANCE AND CONTINUED GROWTH.** One of the best living tuba players, Rex Martin, believes that striving to grow is best. He said, "If you're not trying to get better, you're going to get worse."

3 - **CONTINUED GROWTH AND AWARENESS.**

4 - **TEACHING OTHERS.**

> The two things I understand best are stand-up comedy and martial arts. And those things require an ultimate grasp of the truth. You have to be objective about your skills and abilities to compete in both.
>
> — Joe Rogan

FIVE

WHERE

> ### In This Section
> Where you practice affects improvement, and so does the surrounding environment. Learn how to take advantage of both.

You At?

Compass Over Maps

All of the best learning is discovery, even if others have been there before you. Don't be afraid to launch into something without a clear idea of where you're supposed to go, exactly how to get there, or what you might find along the way. Keep your wits about you and you'll figure it out.

The longer our civilization exists without some catastrophic Dark Ages to wipe out information, the easier it becomes to access that information. This is both a boon and a bane. It's a boon for obvious reasons: Googling anything you need to know is an amazing power.

But easy access to information is also a bane because it robs us not only of the *joy* of discovery, but easy access also robs us of that deep sense of ownership we get when we discover solutions on our own, even if a million others have tread that path before us. Discovering solutions on our own provides a much deeper understanding than reading, Googling, or receiving a nugget of knowledge from someone else.

Believe me, the irony of writing this in a book about getting better isn't lost on me, but remember that it's "compass *over* maps," not "compass *instead* of maps."

Whenever you can, think for yourself, boldly go where you haven't gone before, and explore your own *terra incognita* fearlessly with your compass. Take a map, just in case you get lost and run out of supplies.

Mise en Place

Mise-en-place is a term from the art of the chef, a French phrase meaning "put in place." To chefs it means having their cook station completely stocked, with all the tools of their art ready to hand: spices, knives, peelers, whatever. When things get hot and heavy in a busy kitchen, there's no time to hunt for your cracked pepper or your sharpened paring knife.

If you adopt the *mise-en-place* approach in your practice, you can toss off a quick practice session with no setup time. If it takes time to drag out your gear, you're *much* less likely to do it. *Mise-en-place* makes it easy to do some guerilla practice like I mentioned back on page 84.

Mise-en-place will mean different things for different kinds of practice, of course. If you're a musician, you leave out your instruments; others might leave out a bat, or a ball, or a chess board with an ongoing game from some famous match; you might bookmark a bevy of videos over at www.Lynda.com or YouTube to learn from in less than 10 minutes; or maybe your juggling bean bags are out and at the ready. You get the idea.

Take this concept with you when you're out and about, too. Keep whatever tool you need in your pocket so you can to sneak in some guerrilla practice. You might have a dog-eared copy of the latest book of entrepreneurial wisdom in a pocket, or a poem or soliloquy you're trying to memorize, or a snippet of music you need to learn, or a player's stats. Keep it with you and pull it out when you're waiting in line somewhere. That practice time adds up.

Whatever *mise-en-place* means for you, the most important thing is that your tools are quickly and easily available. Do it!

There are no secrets to success. It's all about mise en place.

Frank Jock

Unless you were raised in the woods alone—wolves don't count because they're social animals—you rely on social networks to learn. We are social creatures. There would be little learning without social networks.

Physician and social scientist Nicholas Christakis has done several fascinating studies illuminating the profound influence our social networks have on our behavior. Peers influence a wide range of behaviors: obesity, smoking, drinking, and more pleasant things like happiness. Where you are and who you hang out with matters. Check out Christakis's talk at http://is.gd/awazey.

There are a couple kinds of social pressures: in-group and out-group pressure. Each can benefit your practice. Let's go over them.

OUT-GROUP PRESSURE: One source of out-group pressure we're all bombarded with is media: books, news, shows, and a deluge of advertising. Ignore that kind of manipulation as much as you can.

Another source of out-group pressure is beneficial. It comes from the audience for whatever it is you do: companies have investors, musicians have concert-goers, teachers have students and parents, artists have art collectors, and there are of course fans and critics of every stripe no matter what you do. Out-group pressure will help motivate you to put in the work so you don't let those folks down when it comes time to shine. Out-groups exert vague pressure that motivates but doesn't instruct.

IN-GROUP PEER PRESSURE: *This* is the kind of peer pressure to seek out and pay close attention to. This pressure comes from your mates, your posse, your chums, your colleagues: the small circle of people whose opinions you actually *care* about. You care because they're the people whose opinions are actually informed, and these folks can give you reliable feedback. The fact that you care about and respect their opinions is exactly why this group is the most powerful source of peer pressure.

The more accomplished peers you surround yourself with, the better you get. Peers don't have to be friends, either. Frenemies are great for motivation, especially a frenemy with whom you might have a heated rivalry. It's good to be pushed, just don't let them push you so hard you fall on your face. Learn more about the right balance of this pressure on the next couple pages.

Group Practice

Writers get together to write and critique each others' work; musicians get together to practice as a band, or to just mess around in a jam; athletes train together; chess enthusiasts play, watch, and talk about games. When we want to get really good at something, practice alone—focusing intently on your skills—is crucial, but so is practicing with others.

Practicing with others—especially if they're a little better than you—will push you further and stretch you in ways you probably wouldn't discover on your own. This is especially true for skills like writing and music that are often developed mostly through solitary practice. If you're part of a larger team sport, like football, soccer, or basketball, consider getting together with just one or two other people and training that way. This will give you direct feedback. When you practice with others, here are some good things to keep in mind:

1 - **ESTABLISH GOALS:** Just messing around is a lot of fun and it *will* help you get better, but if you want to get better faster, have a goal for your practice session. It can be your own personal goal (not a bad idea), but even better is a goal that everybody agrees on, so you're all working toward the same thing. A Review of goal-setting tips on page 40 won't hurt.
2 - **MAKE A PLAN:** Having a goal is great, but it'll help even more to have a battle-plan that will enable you to reach those goals. It doesn't have to be formal: just chat about what you're going to do to reach the goal and get to it.
3 - **RECORD IT:** Use video or audio to record what you did. Re-experiencing the practice session from an outside perspective will help solidify what you learned, and will help show you what's working and what isn't.
4 - **REVIEW:** As soon as possible, go over what you just did, either informally for a couple minutes or more in-depth, say with the video or audio you recorded. Identify weaknesses to work on next time.
5 - **REPEAT.**

To squeeze even more juice out of practice with others, check out the next couple pages.

Find the Fast Lane

When we're surrounded by people with more advanced skills than ours, we get better faster because these people help us perform beyond our current ability.

Educational psychologist Lev Vygotsky called the zone we're in when we're with people more skilled than we are, the Zone of Proximal Development. It's the place where we get better *lots* faster.

Learning to speak is a great example of the Zone of Proximal Development (ZPD). As you were learning to speak, you were surrounded by adults who had vastly greater skill at verbal communication than you. You got constant feedback on your efforts to communicate, and you got all kinds of help from various scaffolds designed to boost your understanding and performance. The alphabet song is one of those scaffolds. More on scaffolds below. Being so fully immersed in the ZPD is one reason we pick up language so quickly as children.

Here are few definitions that will help you squeeze more juice out of the ZPD, developed by other educational psychologists who recognized the power of Vygotsky's insights into how we learn best from others:

SCAFFOLDS: A scaffold is some kind of aid, either physical or mental. Examples of physical scaffolds would be using a block in yoga or the tee used in tee-ball. A mental scaffold could be using a mnemonic device to remember the lines of a music staff, or the alphabet song.

FADING: Fading is a gradual process of removing the scaffold as you begin to be able to do the skill on your own.

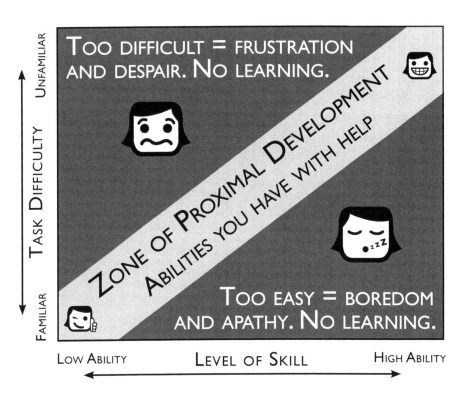

If you're the best person in the room, find another room!

GUIDED LEARNING: Having someone who knows their stuff guide you (and others) through a task can increase how fast you learn something.

RECIPROCAL TEACHING: When you're in a group, it's best if everybody is teaching each other. Not only will you learn from others, you'll learn what you already know even more deeply when you teach others.

So now what do you do?

1 - **CHALLENGE YOURSELF.** If you're not challenged by those around you, you won't improve very quickly. Avoid stroking your ego, and stoke your talent instead by seeking out those better than you. Without being a pest, see if you can hang out with them, or pay them to help you. If you're lucky enough to get the opportunity for guided learning, be humbly respectful and pay attention!
2 - **DON'T REINVENT THE WHEEL.** Find the best learning tools to help you scaffold your learning. Lots of folks have learned what you're learning now. Find out what they used and use that.
3 - **DON'T RELY ON A CRUTCH** or other tool if you don't have to. Start the fading process with a learning tool as soon as you can. On the other hand, if you take away the crutch and fall on your face, it's okay to pick it back up again.
4 - **GIVE BACK** by helping somebody else. Reciprocal teaching is an important aspect of the ZPD. Think back to when you had a great hang with your friends and you all taught each other things. It's like that. When one teaches, two learn.

Every living being is an engine geared to the wheelwork of the universe. Though seemingly affected only by its immediate surrounding, the sphere of external influence extends to infinite distance.

— Nikola Tesla

SIX

Do

> ### IN THIS SECTION
> LEARN WHAT GOOD PRACTICE IS; ITS STRUCTURE AND HOW IT WORKS BEST.
>
> ALSO LEARN USEFUL HACKS TO GET BETTER FASTER.

IT
TO
IT

Tackling the Monster

 That's what Wynton Marsalis calls good practice, because confronting your monstrous weaknesses is daunting, but that's exactly what you have to do. Tackling a monster without a plan isn't a very good idea, though. Knowing what good practice looks like will help you defeat the dragon.

Think of practice as three phases that loop around in a continuous cycle, like the *ouroboros*, the dragon swallowing its own tail.

Here are the parts to the bigger-picture of the practice cycle:

1 - **Prepare:** Review your goals, have a plan to reach the goals, and even specific tactics to get a necessary skill under your belt. This can be detailed and written down, or done informally on the fly.
2 - **Do it:** The meat and potatoes. There is also a useful flow to this part of the practice cycle, the details of which are on the next pages.
3 - **Reflect:** Usually, you'll do this informally, reviewing the session to see how it went, what worked, what didn't, and why. Sometimes you might record it or take detailed notes on how it went. All of that information then feeds into the beginning of the cycle, so....
4 - **Repeat.**

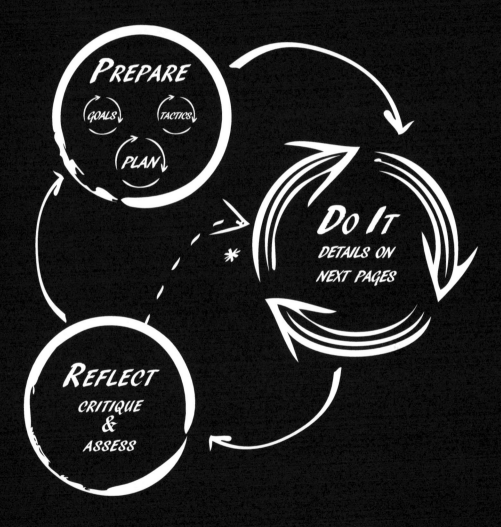

* Critique is ongoing. It's done not only after practice, but during it, too, feeding back into the practice session. For more, see "Check Yourself (Before you Wreck Yourself)" on page 111.

START ➡

WARM-UP
MENTAL & PHYSICAL*
WHAT NEEDS WORK?

PREPARE
GOALS, TACTICS, PLAN

REFLECT
Review. What worked?
What didn't work?
Evaluate & assess

PLAY‡
USE NEW SKILLS

‡ Occasional: full run-throughs and/or performance-level play isn't usually part of practice. When it is, focus on incorporating the new skills.

IDEAL PRACTICE STRUCTURE

BUILD NEW SKILLS
DRILLS, EXERCISES, STRENGTHEN, SLOW SPEED, REPETITION

FOCUS ON ACCURACY, CORRECT FORM

✱ The best warm-up reflects the practice session to come. Use aspects of the practice session in the warm-up. Warm-up *is* practice. Or it should be.

INCORPORATE NEW SKILLS
USE NEW SKILLS IN "REAL" SITUATIONS

FOCUS ON ACCURACY, CORRECT FORM, PERFORMANCE SPEED

CHECK YOURSELF
(BEFORE YOU WRECK YOURSELF)

You have limited brain-power. One reason most experts only put in 2-4 hours of daily practice is that they're focused with laser-like intensity on what they're doing. One of the brain-drains in good practice comes from assessment: being hyper-aware of *all* the details so you know you're doing it right. Ongoing assessment is one of the most important parts of practice, one that isn't mentioned often enough. Assessment comes in two flavors: summative and formative.

SUMMATIVE ASSESSMENT sums up everything you've been working on into one, neat, incomplete-but-informative package. It's the SAT, the championship game, closing the epic deal, the Carnegie Hall performance, the big race; summative assessment is the clinch moment when you either succeed or you realize you have to get back to work.

Relying only on summative assessment to chart your progress is a sucker's game because so much is at stake. Even a small failure could be disastrous. You don't start base-jumping by stuffing a parachute in a backpack and jumping off a cliff and hope it goes well. You take lots of baby steps and assess those smaller steps *long* before you jump off the cliff. I mean, at least start by jumping off a bridge, right? That's where formative assessment comes in.

FORMATIVE ASSESSMENT is all of the little assessments that let you know you're ready to jump off the cliff. The more formative assessment you get, the better. It's called "formative" assessment because you're forming the skill, you're building it up, and as it comes together, you need to monitor your progress to make sure everything is going swimmingly. These assessments should take place in every single practice session. Refer back to the diagrams starting on page 107.

It's the formative assessment that drains your brain during practice. Formative assessment allows you to:

...tell whether you're practicing correctly.
...monitor and see progress and improvement.
...identify weaknesses.
...plan improvement strategies.
...realign your goals, especially immediate-, micro-, and nano-goals.

So now what do you do?

In general, assessment is ongoing and informal, which means you don't have to write it down or go out of your way to do it, but it wouldn't hurt, especially at first. Those who want to get good really fast usually do some or all of the following :

1 - **SET EASILY MEASURED GOALS.** If you don't have a goal, you don't know what you need to assess. Set small, easily-achieved, and easily-measured goals. Review goals on page 37 and page 40.
2 - **RECORD THE SESSION.** Keep track of what you're doing. Most experts keep a log-book, or a diary, or some sort of practice record. Keep it quick and dirty so it's not a chore. Include what you did and whether it worked or not, and what you need to do next as well as how you're going to do it. On special occasions or for extra oomph, record using sound or video so you can really dig in with your assessment.
3 - **CRAFT A RUBRIC.** A rubric is guide or checklist for specific skills telling you exactly how a skill is to be evaluated. If you make it a simple checklist, you can quickly assess your progress and discover what needs more work.
4 - **GET SOME HELP.** Strangers, coaches, teachers, and especially peers will give you more insight into your progress. Choose wisely: you want someone who will keep it real, giving you honest, *useful* feedback. Grandmas will give you cookies, but will probably *not* give you useful critiques. A good coach or teacher is especially helpful because they will also tell you how to correct problem issues.

Sometimes it helps to have gadgets to record what you're doing for later analysis, especially with a coach, teacher, or other expert. Here's one excellent option:

COACH'S EYE: This app allows you to upload and analyze video. The app has lots of great tools, and for a few bucks a month you can unlock other powerful analytics and cloud-based functions. Learn more at http://is.gd/ewiyiq.

Honest criticism is tough to hear, especially if it's from a friend, a relative, an acquaintance, or a total stranger.

— Franklin P. Jones

CREATIVE PRACTICE

Ditch the Quiver

Lars Anderson can fire three arrows in about a half-second, he can jump and catch an arrow in the air and fire it before hitting the ground, and he can hit an incoming arrow that was shot at him. In one of many creative moves contrary to conventional archery wisdom, Anderson got rid of his quiver because he discovered that it got in the way.

Here's the thing: Lars Anderson learned his incredible skills by being creative with his practice. Creativity is an essential component to good practice, but despite the importance of creativity, it's a trait that's often ignored when we think about practice.

One way to boost creativity in practice is to ignore the way it's "supposed" to be done, and try things out on your own. At the very least, you should investigate *why* things are supposed to be done a certain way. You might find that it's true, or you might find a better way. Lars Anderson discovered he could fire more arrows more accurately if he got rid of his quiver and held his arrows in his draw hand. Compass over maps.

With a creative approach, and tons of practice, Anderson also learned to draw with his arrows on the "wrong" side of the bow; to shoot accurately (and fast!) with either hand; and he even learned to catch an arrow shot at him and shoot it back. Don't believe it? Check out the video: http://is.gd/atikas.

A creative approach to practice will not only allow you to discover new techniques like Anderson did, creativity will keep you *engaged* with your practice, and it'll help you to really, truly, deeply *own* your practice. When you discover something on your own, even if a hundred million others have discovered it before you, that sense of discovery is still electrifying, motivating, and golden.

So what does it mean to practice creatively? Glad you asked. In addition to interrogating conventional wisdom in your field, try the ideas on the next pages.

So now what do you do?

1. - **Practice constraint:** Unlimited possibility overwhelms a creative approach. Set tight limits to help boost your creativity. Dr. Seuss was challenged to write a book using less than 50 words, not including repetition, of course. He wrote *Green Eggs and Ham*.
2. - **Kill your apathy**: Maintain a sense of play, irreverence, and silliness. When your practice is tedious and repetitive, try to make it fun by inventing games, doing it with the lights off, or something equally unexpected or wacky, like taking off your shoes. Jazz trumpeter Clark Terry was a playful man who could play his trumpet upside down, fingering with the backs of his knuckles, and he could play two trumpets at once. We learn best when having fun. It's what kids do. You should, too.
3. - **Get two-faced:** Einstein, van Gogh, Pasteur, Picasso, and many others use this technique. When tackling a tough problem, especially if you're stuck, think about it from another perspective, approach it from a different angle, or imagine the problem's polar opposite.
4. - **Get some distance:** Imagine yourself a year from now. How would future-you deal with the problem you're now facing? How would you teach the solution of this problem to a ten-year-old version of yourself?
5. - **Role-play:** Pretend you're an expert, I mean *really* adopt that persona and tackle something you're struggling with in practice. Imagine what that expert would do to overcome the problem. You can role-play as a general expert, but it's best to imagine somebody you admire and know a lot about. If I'm working on didgeridoo, I might imagine I'm Ondrej Smeykal. When I'm struggling with my lifelong goal of being able to hang 10 on a longboard, I'd probably imagine I'm Chelsea Williams, or Harley Ingleby. Check out world longboard champion Chelsea Williams at http://is.gd/ajekiy.
6. - **Choose your own adventure:** Your challenges and your mistakes are unique, and because of this, you'll need to invent your own exercises to address the stuff you're working on. Ethan Bensdorf, trumpeter with the New York Philharmonic, says that when he runs up against problems, he invents exercises to fix them. You should, too. Creativity makes practice more fun, and it works.

A FIRST-RATE SOUP IS MORE CREATIVE THAN A SECOND-RATE PAINTING.

ABRAHAM MASLOW

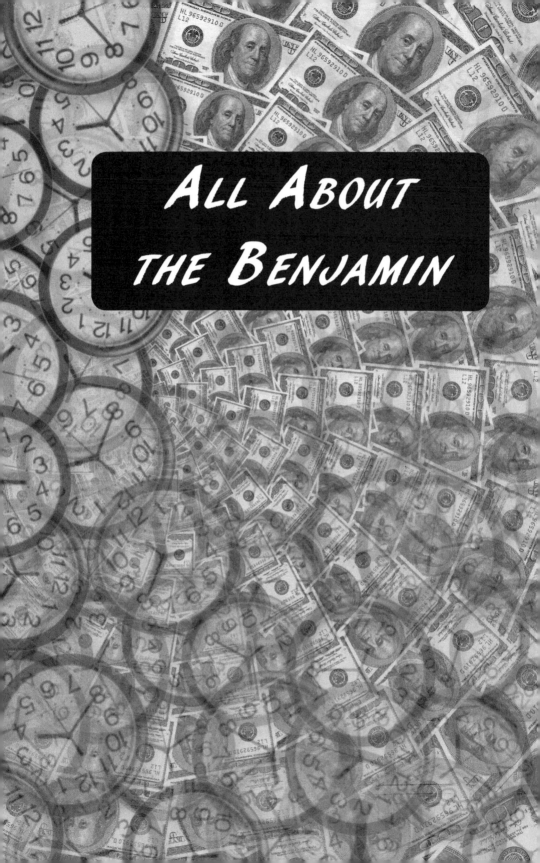

THE IMITATION GAME

Benjamin Franklin invented the mail system, bifocals, lightning rods, the Franklin stove, the first map of the Gulf stream, swim fins, the glass harmonica, a flexible catheter, and odometers, among other useful things. Franklin was also an excellent and prolific writer. From his autobiography, we know that one way Franklin taught himself to write well was by using focused imitation. You can use it too, no matter what you're practicing. Here's how Franklin did it:

1 - **SELECT A MODEL.** Choose a great example of what you'd like to be able to do. Franklin chose writing but this can work with just about anything: music, sculpture, a marketing plan, a recipe, etc.
2 - **SUM IT UP.** Jot down hints, outline, or impressions of the finished product, so you know generally what you're after. Set those hints aside for a few days.
3 - **DO IT ON YOUR OWN.** Re-create the thing as closely as you can, but using your own style, words, sound, or whatever.
4 - **TRANSLATE IT INTO ANOTHER FORM.** Franklin would write essays in verse, then put the verse back into essay form. Generally, get creative with the material. Draw it, mime it, or whatever. Change it up in some way, then change it back to the original.
5 - **JUMBLE UP THE HINTS:** take the hints you created in #2 and jumble them up. See if you can re-create an order that makes sense from the jumbled hints.
6 - **COMPARE:** how does your effort measure up to the original?
7 - **REVISE AND IMPROVE**: take those comparisons and use them to revise and improve what you've already done.
8 - **REPEAT AS MOTIVATION ALLOWS.**
9 - **START COPYING A NEW MODEL.**

THOSE WHO DO NOT WANT TO IMITATE ANYTHING, PRODUCE NOTHING.

SALVADOR DALÍ

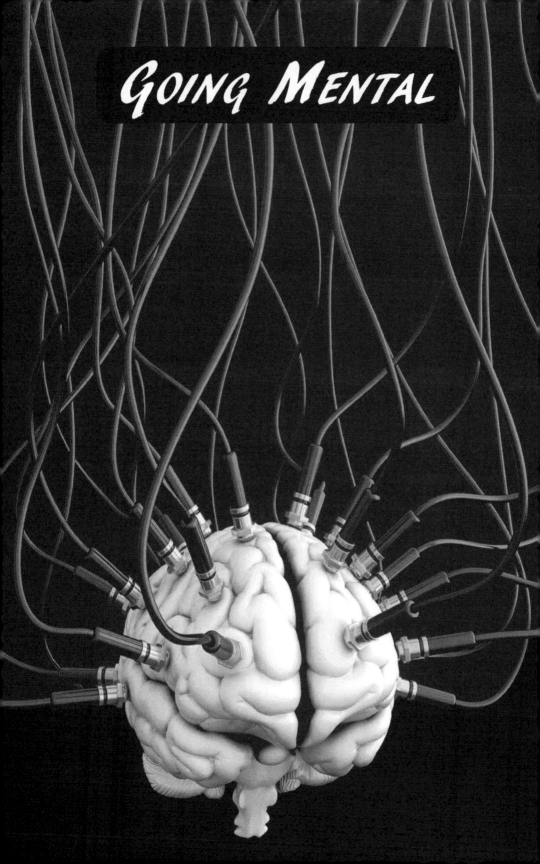

World Champion Formula 1 race car driver Jenson Button sits with his eyes closed on a large purple exercise ball, a steering wheel gripped loosely in front of him. In his mind, he's doing a lap, tapping out the gear changes in real time. When he opens his eyes, he checks to see if his inner time is the same as his real lap time.

Button isn't alone doing this kind of precisely imagined mental practice. Surgeons do it, speakers and presenters do it, sports icons do it, legendary musicians do it, and *you* should do it. Mental practice comes in lots of flavors, not just imagining physical movements. Check it out:

1 - **Self-talk:** During practice, talking to yourself isn't a sign you're crazy, it's a sign of self-coaching and is a technique used by top performers in all fields. Self-talk is especially useful when you're having trouble with something. When you talk yourself through it, keep these tips in mind:

   * "You" statements are more effective than "I" statements.
   * Stay positive, use short focused statements related to the task.
   * Have a cue phrase or statement and use it consistently (mine is "Okay, now you need to...").
   * Identify problems and their solutions out loud as specifically as you can.
   * Don't be shy about trying all of these several times, until you talk yourself through the problem.

2 - **Note card reminders:** Carry around a small notebook or 3x5 note cards with crucial information on them. Pull them out during the day for a quick mental review. Focus on only one thing, then go back to whatever you were doing.

3 - **The Watcher:** Imagine someone you admire is in the room with you, paying close attention to what you're doing. Putting up a poster or picture of the person helps, as does imagining the esteemed person is right behind you, watching and assessing your every move.

4 - **Imaginate:** Create a mental performance like Jenson Button does. Include *every single detail* you can imagine. Visit the place you'll perform in to help you see, feel, hear, smell and taste the performance space. Once you envision the space and audience, imagine every single move you have to make. *Feel* the instrument or the bat or the ball and the clothes you're wearing. Mentally perform *every* move you have to make in exquisite detail.

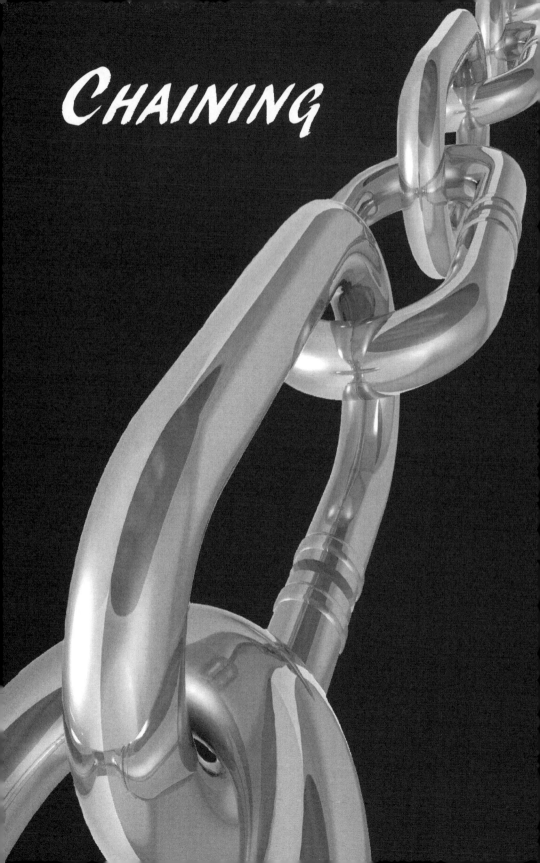

To harness the chaining strategy, break a skill down into small components, or links in the chain, then take each link and practice *only* that one small link and its transitions. Gradually string the links together.

Just like chains are linked, you want to link your actions together, too, with transitions. To do this, include a snippet of what comes both before and after the link you're working on. Your ultimate goal is a seamless flow through the entire motion or passage of music or whatever you're improving, and transitions will help the entire skill become seamless.

Here's the sequence for chaining practice:

1 - **BREAK THE SKILL DOWN** into small components with transitions.
2 - **START AT THE BEGINNING.** Go slowly.
3 - **ISOLATE AND PRACTICE EACH STEP** throughout the task first before combining them.
4 - **COMBINE SUCCESSIVE LINKS** for longer repetitions.
5 - **PRACTICE THE ENTIRE SKILL**, moving fluidly through all components.
6 - **INCREASE SPEED AND REPEAT** until the skill is mastered.

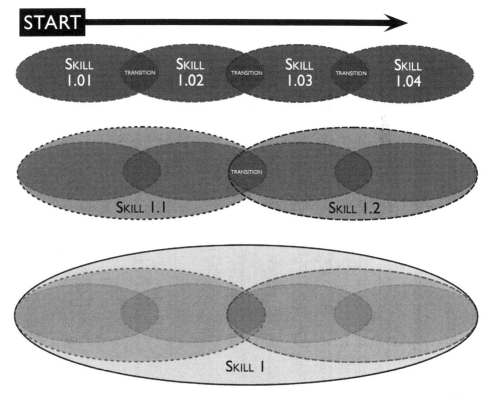

Sometimes you need to finish strong, and in most cases, the finish is when you're at your weakest, so finishing strong can be a challenge. Use back-chaining to overcome this weakness. Back-chaining results in more repetitions of those crucial final steps.

Back-chaining is simply reversing the chaining idea: you start from the end and work your way to the beginning, looping a small portion of the movement or section you're working on. By the time you've made it to the beginning, that last component has received the most repetitions.

Of course, even though you're working backwards through the material you aren't actually *doing* it backwards, Each component is still done forwards, you're just putting the *sequence* backwards.

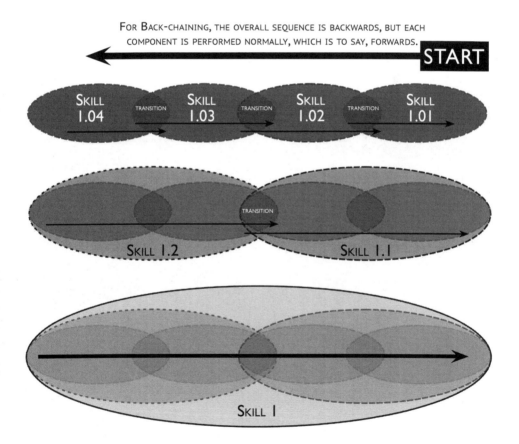

BACK-CHAINING

Lulled in the countless chambers of the brain, our thoughts are linked by many a hidden chain. Awake but one, and lo, what myriads rise! Each stamps its image as the other flies.

—Alexander Pope

Playing With Time

The way your brain learns is by building the neural connections necessary to do whatever it is you're practicing. This is particularly challenging when what you're trying to learn is much faster than you can actually do it. You have to slow time down in order to learn the skill correctly.

If you frequently do something incorrectly during practice, *that's* what your brain remembers. The processes in your brain are mechanical and, ironically, mindless. That's why *you* have to be smart. Take your time. Do it right. Review myelin on page 20 to remind yourself.

Gradually speeding up an ability is the logical, rational way to approach a skill that needs speeding up. You can do it just by feel, but if it makes sense, use a metronome for extra precision, even if you're not a musician.

Using a metronome not only allows you to keep track of your speed over time, it'll point out where your rhythm isn't as precise as you thought, and it allows you to increase speed by very small, nearly imperceptible increments. Here's how it works:

1 - **Find the speed** at which you can accurately do whatever you're trying to do. Pay close attention to how relaxed you are. If you can do it, but are tense, or on the verge of making a mistake, keep repeating it until you're relaxed. To get something super fast, you *have* to be relaxed. Practice that way.

2 - **Increase the tempo just enough** so you creep into the zone where you're not comfortable any more, are still able to do the skill correctly, but you're at the edge of making a mistake. One or two clicks on a metronome is probably enough. Review the Flow diagram on page 47. You're shooting for the "arousal" zone.

3 - **Keep repeating** the skill until you're relaxed and comfortable again. A metronome isn't essential. Hand claps or counting rhythmically works, but if the action is timed precisely you'll keep track better.

4 - **Repeat.**

This is the best way to increase your speed for tasks with performance speeds that are well beyond your capability. For tasks with performance speeds that *are* within your capability, you can benefit from another, even faster method to reach performance speed. Curious? Turn the page.

A More Advanced Way to Play With Time

The method below has been shown to produce quicker and more solid improvement than the gradually-speeding-up method, but to use this method, the performance speed has to be within your reach.

If the ultimate performance speed of your task is beyond you, I'd suggest using the method on the previous page. You could tweak this method by setting a goal that is at the bleeding edge of your ability—even if it's not the actual final speed—and use that as your temporary "performance speed."

This method also involves going *very* slowly, so slowly that you're perfectly relaxed and performing whatever it is you're working on with perfect form. No errors of *any* kind. This is harder than it sounds.

The method is easy. Here are the steps:

1 - **Go slowly:** Perform the task (motion, musical passage, golf swing, elevator pitch, whatever) slowly enough that you're relaxed, your form is perfect, and you're not making even a tiny mistake. Repeat several times.
2 - **Full speed:** Now perform the task at performance speed, whatever that is for the task you're practicing. It might be a total mess, an absolute disaster. That's okay. You're training your body and mind to learn what performance speed feels like. If it *is* an absolute disaster, don't do more than a couple repetitions so you don't encode the mistakes.
3 - **Evaluate & assess.** Where did it work? Where did it fail, and most importantly, why?
4 - **Repeat.** Go slowly and accurately again, focused on the aspect that worked least well at full speed (this may well be *all* of it).

Who forces time is pushed back by time; who yields to time finds time on their side.

The Talmud

LET'S GET PHYSICAL

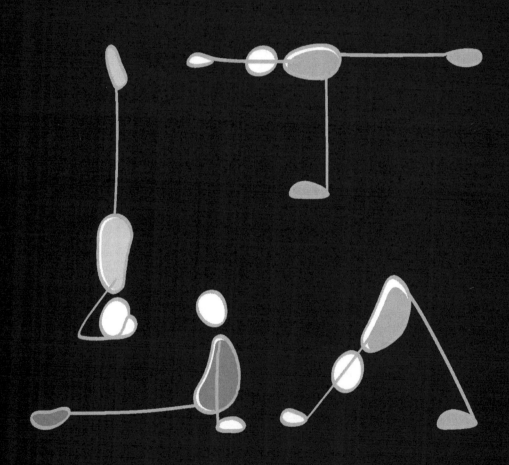

There is a clear link between physical and mental relaxation and increased performance. The more relaxed and efficient the body and mind, the better everything works. Many athletes, musicians, writers, and actors study disciplines that train them how to hold themselves correctly. A good example is six-foot-four, 320-pound NFL nose tackle Steve McLendon, who studies ballet.

McLendon says ballet helps keep him on his toes and injury-free by strengthening his knees, ankles, and feet. More famous NFL players like Herschel Walker and Lynn Swann studied ballet, too. I leave it to you to insert your own hilarious Swann Lake pun here.

In addition to ballet or a martial art, there are a few other less physically rigorous options to train your body in order to boost your abilities. If you're interested, you can probably find a teacher of one of these methods near you. Take a lesson or two.

We're all familiar with the benefits of plain old physical exercise, and many of us know about the benefits of yoga. Here are a two less-well-known disciplines that help musicians, actors, and athletes:

The Alexander Technique: The Alexander Technique centers around how you hold your head, your chest, and your hips. Generally, the idea is to let the skeletal structure do the "work" in staying upright, allowing you to move in a relaxed, open way. Artists who use the Alexander Technique include Paul McCartney, Sting, Ben Kingsley, Judi Dench, Roald Dahl, Aldous Huxley, and a whole host of other superbly talented individuals. Check out a large collection of videos explaining the basics of the Alexander technique at http://is.gd/donodu.

Feldenkreis Method: Martial artist Moshé Feldenkrais developed techniques to help people become conscious of their movement. There are over 2,000 exercises and techniques used to focus one's awareness on the ways in which the body moves. The Feldenkreis Method is also used by many artists and athletes. Learn more about it at http://is.gd/demufi.

One of the most overlooked factors to getting better quickly is the power of sleep, and not just night-time sleep, but naps, too. High-level performers know this and many of them nap regularly, especially after the heavy practice session of the day. The scientific record is crystal clear on the subject: better sleep means better performance on all levels.

We all know the power of a good night's sleep, but it may have been a year or ten since you had nap-time. Taking naps isn't a sign of laziness or immaturity, it's a power-up. Knowing the stages of sleep will help you hone your nap-jitsu. This cycle repeats during sleep, roughly every 90 minutes.

STAGE 1: Falling asleep. A hypnogogic state that some people (Dalí, Edison, etc.) have used productively for its free-floating association which can foster creative insight. It's the least-understood kind of sleep.

STAGE 2: In this stage, brainwaves become "rhythmic," producing electrical patterns that strengthen neuronal connections. Stage Two sleep is important for learning physical movements (motor memory), the steps of how to do something (procedural memory), and implicit memory, or things you learn without consciously trying, like remembering how to get somewhere new.

STAGE 3 & 4: This deeper sleep is called Delta sleep, or slow-wave sleep (SWS) because the brain produces slow Delta waves during these stages. This stage helps the body repair itself, like after a tough workout. Neural activity is minimal, which may help clear the brain/mind of useless memories. These stages are vital for declarative memory, which is remembering consciously learned things, like facts.

STAGE 5: This stage is known as REM sleep (rapid eye movement). Dreams are most vivid in REM sleep. There is a link between REM sleep and memory improvement, as well as evidence that REM sleep plays a role in transferring important short-term memories to long-term memory. REM sleep is also crucial for building emotional memories. Perceptual skills are solidified in this stage. Finally, REM sleep is associated with a boost in creativity and heightened sensory perceptions like hearing, touch, taste, smell, etc.

Hack Your Nap-Time

As you can see from the list above, each stage of sleep replenishes certain skills, so depending on your needs, you can tweak your nap to help produce the benefits you desire. If you're working on your improv comedy chops, dreaming up a business or marketing plan, or writing songs, you'll want a nap with more REM sleep, because REM sleep boosts creativity. If you're learning new drills, new music, or other physical skills, you want a nap with stage 2 sleep. You get the idea, right?

Here's some final advice to help you get the most out of your nap:

LENGTH: A nap doesn't have to be long. Five minutes is about the shortest length, but most experienced nappers put in around 20 minutes of shut-eye. More isn't always better where naps are concerned. A 60-minute nap will put you into phase 4 sleep which will leave you fuzzy-headed for a while after waking from it. If you want a long nap, shoot for 45 minutes (or 90 minutes, as this will give you a full sleep cycle). If you can't commit to that kind of time, a shorter nap might be better. Knowing more about sleep stages will help you get the most out of your nap time. The only book you need is Sara Mednick's *Take a Nap!* (link is below).

TIME OF DAY: Optimal nap time is around 1-3 in the afternoon, but it depends on when you woke up and how much "sleep debt" you've built up. If you can, nap after your main practice session. A strategically placed nap allows your brain to consolidate and store the important stuff you've been practicing, and at the same time, wipes the slate clean so you're ready to take in more, later in the day. Use Mednick's "Nap Wheel" to find out the best nap time. It's in her book, but you can find one free online at http://is.gd/otogeh (it's a Flash animation so it won't work on Apple computer devices).

NAP-JITSU: Research shows that getting prone is best for naps, and it's a good idea to cover yourself with a light blanket because your body temperature drops when you're asleep. Comfy isn't absolutely necessary but will help. Try a nap-app like *SleepCycle* or *SleepBot* to dial in the correct time for your nap. For some added *zoom* when you wake up, try swilling coffee or some other caffeinated beverage just before you nod off, as it takes around 45 minutes for caffeine to hit your brain.

EXTRA-CREDIT
This talk by Jeff Iliff covers how the brain cleans itself out with cerebrospinal fluid during sleep. See the talk at http://is.gd/mihedu.

It is a common experience that a problem difficult at night is resolved in the morning after the committee of sleep has worked on it.

John Steinbeck

In theory, there is no difference between theory and practice. In practice, there is.

— Yogi Berra

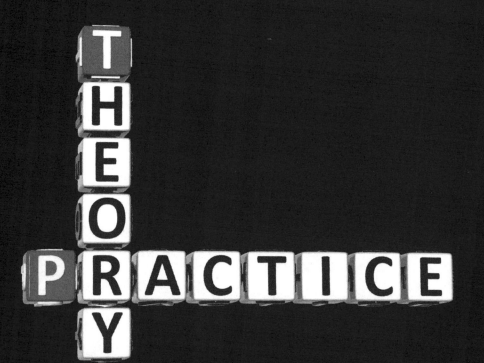

At the Buzzer

We all have different challenges, different goals, and different life experiences. This means you'll probably find that some techniques in this book work great, and some, not so much. Like the advertisement says, "Your results may vary." No matter what you're learning, always seek other sources. I won't be jealous, I promise.

As you start using and experimenting with the ideas in this book, keep in mind these wise words from everybody's favorite martial arts master:

Absorb what is useful. Discard what is not. Add what is uniquely your own.

—Bruce Lee

Whatever skills you're trying to master, you have my best wishes for your continued (and continuous) improvement. Come say hello online over at: www.PracticeLikeThis.com.

—Jon

OTHER BOOKS BY JONATHAN HARNUM

SOL UT PRESS
WWW.SOL-UT.COM

Basic Music Theory
How to Read, Write, and Understand Written Music (4th edition)

What do all those lines and squiggles and dots mean? *Basic Music Theory* takes you through the sometimes confusing world of written music with a clear, concise style that is at times funny and always friendly. Includes comprehensive chapter and section reviews and hundreds of online examples (226 pages).

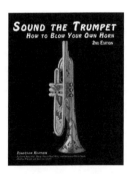

Sound the Trumpet
How to Blow Your Own Horn (2nd edition)

Packed with information no trumpet player should be without. Learn to master basic skills like lip slurs, buzzing, and breathing. Covers more advanced skills like double- and triple-tonguing, transposing, cool sound effects, how to play high, endurance, and many other helpful skills. Includes hundreds of online examples and freebies (274 pages).

The Practice of Practice
How to Boost Your Music Skills

This book tackles music practice specifically. The stories and the science inside were drawn from Harnum's in-depth interviews with world-class musicians in multiple genres of music and published research on practice. While much of the information is similar to what you've read in *Get Better Faster*, concepts are explored more fully, and include music-specific strategies and techniques for getting better (274 pages).

Made in the USA
Columbia, SC
19 July 2021